FARNHAM SCHOOL OF ART

FARNHAM SCHOOL OF

KV-613-917

2 4 SEP 2010

WITHDRAWN
FROM STOCK

THE COMMONWEALTH AND INTERNATIONAL LIBRARY

Joint Chairmen of the Honorary Editorial Advisory Board

SIR ROBERT ROBINSON, O.M., F.R.S., LONDON

DEAN ATHELSTAN SPILHAUS, MINNESOTA

Publisher: ROBERT MAXWELL, M.C., M.P.

LIBRARIES AND TECHNICAL INFORMATION DIVISION

General Editor: G. CHANDLER

HOW TO FIND OUT ABOUT
THE WOOL TEXTILE INDUSTRY

HOW TO FIND OUT ABOUT
THE WOOL TEXTILE INDUSTRY

by

HUGO LEMON

PERGAMON PRESS

OXFORD · LONDON · EDINBURGH · NEW YORK

TORONTO · SYDNEY · PARIS · BRAUNSCHWEIG

Pergamon Press Ltd., Headington Hill Hall, Oxford
4 & 5 Fitzroy Square, London W.1

Pergamon Press (Scotland) Ltd., 2 & 3 Teviot Place, Edinburgh 1

Pergamon Press Inc., 44–01 21st Street, Long Island City, New York 11101

Pergamon of Canada Ltd., 207 Queen's Quay West, Toronto 1

Pergamon Press (Aust.) Pty. Ltd., 19a Boundary Street,
Rushcutters Bay, N.S.W. 2011, Australia

Pergamon Press S.A.R.L., 24 rue des Écoles, Paris 5ᵉ

Vieweg & Sohn GmbH, Burgplatz 1, Braunschweig

Copyright © 1968 Pergamon Press Ltd.
First edition 1968
Library of Congress Catalog Card No. 68–8869

Printed in Great Britain by A. Wheaton and Co., Exeter

FARNHAM SCHOOL OF ART

677.3109 LEM

This book is sold subject to the condition
that it shall not, by way of trade, be lent,
resold, hired out, or otherwise disposed
of without the publisher's consent,
in any form of binding or cover
other than that in which
it is published.

08 012983 8 (flexicover)
08 012984 6 (hard cover)

8179

Contents

Chapter 4. Research for the Wool Textile Industry

Chapter 5. Wool Processing

CHAPTER 6. DISTRIBUTION OF THE WOOL TEXTILE INDUSTRY

List of Illustrations

Foreword

HUGO LEMON's book fulfils a very real demand. All industries need a well-informed introduction, written by an author who can describe the technicalities in words that a layman can understand. It would seem to many that the wool textile industry is in particular need of such a book.

The conversion of wool into cloth is a long, involved process with its own peculiar technical background and its own very peculiar terminology, that can make things even more difficult for the layman. An additional difficulty is the division of the industry into the two sections—woollen and worsted. Judging from the questions that are asked when one is lecturing about wool, this division is mysterious to many people. All these points are clearly and carefully defined in this book.

Another very valuable section is the chapters that detail the various organizations within and concerned with the industry. Such information has not been so clearly stated in any other publication, and is of real value because these organizations play such a necessary part in an industry comprising so many sections.

No one is better equipped than Mr. Lemon to write this introduction. Whilst he was at the Wool Industries Research Association, many scientists and other authors profited from his editorial advice and assistance. It is indeed a pleasure to recommend this book to all who are interested in the wool textile industry.

As one of Britain's oldest industries its history is, in many ways, the economic history of England; and today, despite the competition of other fibres, it remains very important, particularly as a major exporter of high quality fabrics to all parts of the world.

K. G. PONTING,
Chairman of the Wool Textile Research Council

Preface

THIS book is intended to be of some use to any one who is interested in any aspect of wool and its processing. During my time
as editor for the Wool Industries Research Association, when I
was concerned also with public relations and press liaison, I
often felt the need for a source of information that would either
provide the answers to the many queries that came my way or
would indicate where they should be sought. The present book
would have been a useful desk companion for me, and I hope that
it will prove to be serviceable to others.

The modern wool textile industry is advancing steadily in its
methods and organization, absorbing all that science and technology have to offer. The march of progress will thus inevitably
result in parts of the book becoming out of date sooner or later;
so wherever possible the address is given of an authority from
whom the latest information can be obtained. This contingency
applies particularly to education. It is appreciated that textile
courses must be revised from year to year; the object of giving
some details in Chapter 1 of the current courses being offered is to
indicate the general scope of the courses at the various universities and technical colleges.

I am indebted to a large number of people who have provided
me with the latest information on the educational establishments
and other organizations referred to in the following pages. They
have taken a great deal of trouble, too, in reading the relevant
parts of the text in typescript and commenting helpfully on them.
Individual acknowledgement of their assistance is unfortunately
not practicable.

I should, however, like to express my gratitude to Alan Brearley,
Head of the Department of Textiles at Dewsbury and Batley
Technical and Art College, for much valuable advice, both direct

and through the medium of his books. I am grateful to Dr. A. B. D. Cassie, recently Director of Research at the Wool Industries Research Association, and to my other erstwhile colleagues on the staff there, from whom I learnt over the course of the years enough to enable me to tackle this book; Peter Day, the Wira librarian, has been most helpful. In my search for information on books the librarian and staff of the Kendal and Westmorland Library Service have never failed to supply the answer to a reasonable inquiry, and have succeeded with many that were unreasonable. I have benefited greatly from the knowledge and experience of my son, Christopher Lemon. In spite of all this assistance, so readily given, any errors or omissions that may remain in the book must be laid to the account of the author.

Finally, it is a source of deep gratification to me that Kenneth G. Ponting, Chairman of the Wool Textile Research Council, with whom I have had so many stimulating discussions, should have consented to give his blessing to my book.

CHAPTER I

Education

CHOICE OF CAREERS

In the modern wool textile industry there is a remarkably wide and varied range of careers available for all types of young people of both sexes. There are jobs for craftsmen, technicians, technologists, scientists, engineers, artists, accountants, social workers, and many more.

The first job that has to be done in the industry is to buy the wool, which is grown in many countries, including the United Kingdom. Some wool merchants specialize in a particular section of the industry such as woollen or worsted, others deal in speciality hair fibres, processing wastes, and other material. Some topmakers in the worsted industry buy raw wool, sort it according to their customers' requirements, and have it combed by commission combers, not having on their own machines. Other firms are merely brokers. The industry recognizes about 7000 grades of wool, each having some particular properties and uses in manufacturing. A wide knowledge of wool and long experience are therefore required, and a wool buyer is often a director of his firm. There are courses at technical colleges designed to prepare students for the job of buyer trainee; alternatively, a buyer may start as a wool sorter, or a suitably educated boy may be taken into the office of a wool merchant and receive his practical training there.

Similar backgrounds lead to careers as salesmen employed by merchants to sell their products both at home and abroad; other firms employ yarn and cloth salesmen. There are thus good opportunities for those who have a flair for languages.

On the manufacturing side the wide scope for craftsmen and technologists will be appreciated from the sections of this book dealing with the various processes, and also with the sections on the Textile Institute, and the City and Guilds of London Institute. The particulars of the courses offered by the textile departments of the universities and technical colleges given below also illustrate the opportunities for careers to suit many different types of young people. Increasing importance is being attached to testing and quality control, and all that is implied by work study, at every stage of mechanical and chemical processing; technological, mathematical, statistical, and other skills are required at various levels of training and education for these activities. Research graduates are being employed in increasing numbers by firms in the industry and by such organizations as the Wool Industries Research Association, the International Wool Secretariat, the Management Services Centre, and others. Training officers are employed in factories and by the Wool, Jute, and Flax Industry Training Board.

Textile design is another skill that is absorbing increasing numbers in the industry. In a small firm, design may be doubled with another occupation, and the designer may be a manager. Larger firms have design departments in which copyists and colourists are employed.

Some factories employ personnel officers whose training may have started with a diploma or degree course at a university. Junior assistants in these departments may obtain promotion by taking the examinations of the Institute of Personnel Management. On the social side, too, there are jobs as canteen supervisors for both men and women.

Accountants are required to fill many posts both in large firms and groups and in the many organizations concerned with the industry's affairs.

Some particulars are given below of the courses offered by universities and technical colleges with textile departments. The information gives a general idea of the type and scope of training at each establishment, and in some cases the particular section of the industry served, or the particular crafts catered for, is indicated. The details of the courses, however, are liable to change; indeed, an educational establishment serving a forward-looking industry must keep its training schemes and syllabuses constantly under review, and be prepared to adapt the courses to the requirements of that industry. The requirements and regulations of the Textile Institute and of the City and Guilds of London Institute are likewise flexible and are modified from time to time.

A potential student may be able to decide from the information on the following pages which establishment and what general line of technical education is likely to suit his particular requirements. Then, for the reasons given in the foregoing paragraph, he should make further inquiries from his Local Advisory Officer, a Youth Employment Officer, Careers Teacher, or other educational authority. Inquiries concerning individual universities and technical colleges should be sent to the addresses given on the following pages, at the end of each description of an establishment.

Particulars of Textile Institute qualifications are given in Chapter 3.

CITY AND GUILDS OF LONDON INSTITUTE

This Institute, often abbreviated to "City and Guilds", is the largest of the examining bodies in technical education. It prepares syllabuses, holds examinations, and awards certificates for craftsmen, technicians, and others. Wool textiles were among the first subjects for which the Institute offered examinations in 1879, the year following its formation.

The provision of schemes (regulations and syllabuses) in wool textiles is the responsibility of the Advisory Committee for Wool Textile Subjects, this being a joint committee representing the City and Guilds of London Institute and the Yorkshire Council for Further Education. This new Advisory Committee came into being effectively early in 1967, taking over the work of the Institute's own Advisory Committee for Woollen and Worsted

Manufactures. The abbreviation "Advisory Committee" thus now normally refers to the new joint committee.

The Advisory Committee is composed of representatives of educational establishments and organizations, scientific research (Wool Industries Research Association), industry (both employers and unions), the Textile Institute, the Department of Education and Science, the Scottish Education Department, and the Youth Employment Service. It is thus truly representative, embracing Scotland and the west of England as well as the Yorkshire area.

The basic structure of wool schemes has recently been rearranged to meet the requirements of the modern industry; the phasing out of the old structure leaves four craft schemes each of which is matched by a technician's scheme, covering at the appropriate levels the following four subjects: (1) wool textile raw materials, (2) worsted spinning, (3) woollen and worsted weaving and tuning, (4) woollen yarn manufacture.

The Advisory Committee watches the needs of the industry and is prepared to devise further schemes as may be demanded by industrial and educational practices. At the same time the whole question of the proliferation of textile courses, particularly in the Yorkshire region, has to be considered. The new craft scheme in woollen yarn manufacture is an example of a wide variety of occupations being brought together in one course; the number and variety of the few people in each clearly rule out separate specialist courses.

Both the technician and craft schemes are practically biased; the new technician schemes emphasize the importance of practical work in the factory to complement theoretical study, and the final examinations include practical tests. In the craft schemes the whole approach is practical, the factory rather than the class-room being the focus of the course.

The details of these schemes will change from time to time as necessity arises, and are given in the current appropriate pamphlet; the following brief information is taken from the pamphlets current in 1967.

Craft Certificate in Wool Textiles Raw Materials

For wool sorters, sample room, and other personnel requiring a sound basic knowledge of the raw materials used in the wool textile industry.

The subjects of study are raw materials, textile manufacturing processes, and microscopy and testing.

Technician's Certificate in Wool Textiles Raw Materials

For trainee wool buyers, salesmen, and others requiring a good technical knowledge of the raw materials used in the wool textile industry combined with an understanding of commerce. The scheme is divided into intermediate and final stages, and at the appropriate level covers wool and other raw materials and their production, textile processing, testing and microscopy, textiles mathematics, commerce (economics), and mercantile law.

Worsted Spinning Craft Certificate

For prospective worsted spinning overlookers. The syllabus includes English and general studies, textile materials, drawing and spinning (theory and practical), workshop practice, basic mill testing (theory and practical), and textile calculations and elementary textile mechanics.

Technician's Certificate in Worsted Spinning

For prospective overlookers, foremen and departmental managers. The syllabus includes general textiles, raw materials, scouring, carding, combing, worsted drawing and spinning, advanced textile testing, mathematics, general science, mechanics, and workshop practice.

Craft Certificate in Woollen and Worsted Weaving and Tuning

For apprentice loom tuners in the wool textile industry. The syllabus includes general textile manufacture, mechanics, mechanisms and sketching of machine parts, workshop practice, yarn preparation and weaving mechanisms, calculations, analysis and cloth structure, loom tuning.

Technician's Certificate in Woollen and Worsted Weaving

For prospective overlookers, foremen and departmental managers. The curriculum has the three headings: designing course; weaving and tuning course; and finishing course. The syllabuses of the designing course and the weaving and tuning course include cloth structure and analysis, design and colour, textile calculations, textile testing, production and weaving mechanisms, and raw materials.

The syllabus of the finishing course includes various aspects of finishing processes, operational practice and theory, and science (finishing).

Craft Certificate in Woollen Yarn Manufacture

For assistant carding overlookers, mule spinners, ring frame spinners, assistant spinning overlookers, winding foremen, teasing foremen, ragpulling foremen, foremen fettlers, and laboratory testers in woollen mills. The syllabus includes general textile manufacture, woollen yarn manufacture, mechanism and sketching, workshop practice, carding and spinning, and testing.

Technician's Certificate in Woollen Yarn Manufacture

For those aiming at positions of responsibility in woollen yarn manufacture. The syllabus covers general textiles, raw materials, blending and carding, spinning, textile testing, mathematics, general science, mechanics, and workshop practice.

Textile Ancillary Subjects

Examinations are offered on the following textile ancillary subjects:

Mill engineering and services
Industrial organization
Chemistry as applied to the textile industry
Appreciation of colour and design
Textile organization and control

City and Guilds of London Institute Insignia Award in Technology

This award is open to those who have gained a full technological certificate of the Institute or a suitable equivalent and have, by further study, broadened their knowledge of the problems of their industry and have extended their understanding of the scientific principles upon which it is based.

There is no formal examination for the award; particulars of the procedure and conditions may be obtained from the Director (Insignia Award), City and Guilds of London Institute, 76 Portland Place, London, W.1.

Further Information

Inquiries should be addressed to:

City and Guilds of London Institute,
76 Portland Place,
London, W.1.

REGIONAL ADVISORY COUNCILS FOR FURTHER EDUCATION

These councils (known as RACs) represent the co-ordination and co-operation of education and industry, one of their main functions being to plan the provision of further education in their region. Another important function is to provide information about the colleges in the region, and the courses they run.

The addresses of the RACs are:

Northern Advisory Council for Further Education,
5 Grosvenor Villas, Grosvenor Road, Newcastle upon Tyne, 2.

Yorkshire Council for Further Education,
Bowling Green Terrace, Jack Lane, Leeds, 11.

North Western Regional Advisory Council for Further Education,
Africa House, 54 Whitworth Street, Manchester, 1.

West Midlands Advisory Council for Further Education,
   Pitman Buildings, 161 Corporation Street, Birmingham, 4.

East Midlands Regional Advisory Council for Further
Education,
   Robins Wood House, Robins Wood Lane, Aspley,
   Nottingham.

East Anglian Regional Advisory Council for Further
Education,
   County Education Office, Stracey Road, Norwich.

London and Home Counties Regional Advisory Council for
Technological Education,
   Tavistock House South, Tavistock Square, London, W.C.1.

Southern Regional Council for Further Education,
   9 Bath Road, Reading, Berkshire.

South-west Regional Advisory Council for Further Education,
   12 Lower Castle Street, Bristol, 1.

Welsh Joint Education Committee,
   30 Cathedral Road, Cardiff.

UNIVERSITIES AND TECHNICAL COLLEGES* WITH TEXTILE DEPARTMENTS

The Queen's University of Belfast

The Faculty of Applied Science and Technology in this University is associated with the Department of Textile Industries in
the City of Belfast College of Technology in connection with a
degree course in textile technology.

B.Sc. Degree Course in Textile Technology

This is a 4-year course which in 1963–4 replaced one that had
been designated Textile Industries. The scope of the course will be
appreciated from the subjects included in the syllabuses.

* These are arranged in alphabetical order of towns and cities.

First Year. The syllabuses for the first-year subjects in chemistry, mathematics, applied mathematics, physics, and technical drawing are as for the degree courses in applied chemistry.

Second Year. In addition to polymer and colour science, mathematics, applied electricity, and mechanical engineering, the following textile subjects are introduced: (a) the production, processing, and properties of fibres; (b) the preparatory and spinning processes and properties of yarns; (c) the preparatory and manufacturing processes and properties of fabrics; (d) the analysis and testing of fibres, yarns, and fabrics.

Third Year. In addition to mathematics, process instrumentation, and physics, the following topics in industrial administration are introduced: (a) development policy, the implementation of policy, co-ordination of activities within the organization, and social responsibilities of management; (b) sources of finance, financial structure, and disposition of capital and revenue profits; (c) the changing concepts of employer–employee relationships, the personal function and its relationship to other managerial functions, and selecting and training subordinates.

Textile subjects include the theoretical and practical aspects of fibres, yarns, and fabrics. The syllabus also includes practical work on the production of yarns from natural and man-made fibres and on the design and production of simple and compound fabrics.

Fourth Year. The syllabus includes fibre physics, textile testing, and advanced textile technology. In addition, some textile project is undertaken.

Further Information

Inquiries should be addressed to:

Head of the Faculty of Applied Science and Technology,
The Queen's University of Belfast,
Belfast.

THE LIBRARY
West Surrey College of Art and Design

City of Belfast College of Technology

The Department of Textile Industries provides full-time and part-time courses for students employed in the various branches of the textile and clothing industries and their associated trades. The emphasis is on the linen and clothing industries, but the Diploma Course in Textile Technology covers all fibres in the subjects of fibre technology and yarn technology. The Department is associated with the Faculty of Applied Science and Technology of The Queen's University of Belfast, in connection with a 4-year full-time internal B.Sc. degree course.

Full-time Courses

Ordinary National Diploma in Textile Technology. This is a 2-year sandwich course consisting of 6-month periods of full-time attendance alternating with 6-month periods in industry. The subjects studied are fibre technology, yarn technology, fabric technology, textile testing, finishing technology, chemistry, physics, mathematics, engineering science, English, and general studies.

Part-time Courses

Amongst the part-time courses are those for clothing, dress manufacture, warehouse apprentice, knitting, sewing machine engineering, analysis and testing, flax spinning, and linen weaving.

Further information

Inquiries should be addressed to:

> Head of Department of Textile Industries,
> City of Belfast College of Technology,
> Belfast, 1.

Blackburn College of Technology and Design

The Department of Textiles offers classes in a wide variety of subjects most of which are grouped together to constitute courses.

As a general rule students are advised to take these courses because they provide a balanced education, and also lead to the award of recognized qualifications.

The courses cover the necessary theoretical and practical instruction for any of the following qualifications:

The Associate and Licentiate Membership of the Textile Institute

Ordinary National Diploma in Textiles

The College Associateship in Textiles

College Diplomas and Certificates

Ordinary and Higher National Certificates in Textiles

Union of Lancashire and Cheshire Institutes—Certificates in General Textiles, Spinning, and Weaving.

Full-time Courses

ATI Part I Intensive Course. Provides instruction covering the whole field of textile technology up to the level of the Part I examination for ATI.

Ordinary National Diploma. A 2-year course of basic training in general textile technology, including a study of the relevant sciences.

College Associateship Course in Textiles. A 3-year course. During the first 2 years training is given in general textile technology; in the final year students specialize in one branch of the industry.

Sandwich Courses

Higher National Diploma in Textile Technology. A 3-year course (6 months at college, 6 months in industry) with an option to specialize in the third college period.

Part-time Courses

Two main types of part-time courses are available.

(1) *Technological Courses*, which lead to the award of Ordinary and Higher National Certificates and to the Associateship of the Textile Institute.

(2) *Technicians' Courses,* which lead to the award of City and Guilds of London Institute Full Technological Certificates, Union of Lancashire and Cheshire Institute Technicians' Certificates in Spinning and Weaving, and Licentiate Membership of the Textile Institute.

In order to prepare students, who may not have reached the required educational standard, for direct entry into the above courses, specially designed preparatory courses are provided. In addition, the Department arranges such part-time courses as: induction courses for operatives, and specialist courses for loom overlookers, apprentice loom overlookers, and textile testing laboratory assistants.

The School of Art and Design runs a textile design course for industrial apprentices, leading to the City and Guilds Intermediate Examination.

Further Information

Inquiries should be addressed to:

> Head of Department of Textiles,
> Blackburn College of Technology and Design,
> Blackburn.

Bolton Institute of Technology

Although the emphasis in the Textile Department is on cotton, there are classes in a wide variety of textile subjects; students may take a single subject or a combination of subjects arranged in groups to constitute courses. Students are encouraged to take these grouped courses because they provide an education superior to that normally obtainable through the study of single subjects or of a random selection of subjects, and they lead to recognized qualifications.

Full-time Courses

Ordinary National Diploma in General Textiles. A 2-year course providing a sound and broadly based introduction to textile materials and processing, from the fibre to the finished product, together with the mathematics and science necessary for a full appreciation and understanding of the technical subjects.

Higher National Diploma in Yarn and Fabric Production. A 2-year course providing for studies at an advanced level over a more specialized field than the Ordinary National Diploma course. A substantial experimental project is included during the final year. Management studies are introduced in the first year and developed in the final year.

Part-time Courses

The following part-time courses are offered: general course in textiles; Higher National Certificate courses in spinning and weaving; Post Higher National Certificate courses for Part II of the Textile Institute's Examination for Associateship; and technician's courses in yarn production and in weaving (City and Guilds Full Technological Certificate).

Further Information

Inquiries should be addressed to:

Head of Department of Textiles,
Bolton Institute of Technology,
Manchester Road,
Bolton.

The University of Bradford

In 1957 the Bradford Institute of Technology became one of the first eight colleges of advanced technology; and in November 1966, following the recommendations of the Robbins Committee, the College became the University of Bradford. The Prime Minister, Mr. Harold Wilson, was installed as Chancellor, and also became the first Doctor of Technology in Britain.

The Department of Textile Industries

The University has a long tradition of co-operation with the wool textile industry, and (as a college) was a pioneer in advanced sandwich courses. These have been developed with the object of promoting the study of science in relation to its application in industry. During such a course the student spends several periods of about 6 months each, or one single period of a year (for the training of textile technologists), working under supervision in industrial research, development, or production units. The principal aim is to introduce him to the practice of applying scientific analysis to industrial processes. In his final year the student undertakes a project closely related to his specialist study, and this forms the basis of a thesis to be presented as part of his final examination. Time is also allotted to the study of humanities, social science, and administrative subjects, these forming an integral part of the course. The undergraduate course in textile technology has been designed, in close collaboration with leading industrialists, to enable students to take up responsible technological and administrative posts in the textile industry.

Undergraduate Honours Course in Textile Technology

This course entails full-time attendance at the University for 3 academic years with an additional year's industrial training interposed after the second year. Students may be accepted as university-based students, arrangements being made for industrial or professional training; or they may be industry-based, being employed by a firm and sent for a particular course.

During the first 2 years a sound background of textile science is established. The third year comprises practical training in industry. The syllabus for the fourth year covers general textile technology, wool technology, and advanced textile science. General and social studies are included in the syllabuses for the first, second, and fourth years.

The awards are classified as first-, second-, and third-class honours.

Undergraduate Honours Course in Textile Design

This course provides a thorough training in art and design combined with the relevant science and technology of the textile industry, enabling the successful student to obtain a responsible position in industry. It is a 4-year course for university-based or industry-based students (see above), the third year comprising practical training in industry.

Postgraduate Course in Textile Technology

The basic course gives graduates with a scientific background a training in textile physics, textile chemistry, and general textile technology. The syllabus includes the structure and management of the textile industry, fine morphology and identification, textile testing and statistics, textile mathematics, textile materials, man-made fibre technology, conversion of fibres into yarns and yarns into fabrics, structure and properties of fabrics, appreciation of colour, textile engineering, fundamentals of dyeing, and cloth finishing.

Research Fellowships and Research Assistantships

The wool textile industry sponsors a research programme of pure and applied research. Much of the fundamental work involves the latest techniques applicable to physics and chemistry and is suitable for a higher degree. The fellowships and assistantships are intended for graduates (or the equivalent) in textiles, engineering, physics, chemistry, or biology with some research or industrial experience, who wish to extend their knowledge of research techniques or particular fields of research. Fellows and assistants take part in current research, usually on a particular project, the work being suitable for publication and in most cases may be submitted in thesis form for a higher degree. Research fellows and assistants are paid on a salary scale with additional allowances for training and qualifications.

Scholarships are available to suitable applicants: (a) Bradford City Research Scholarships: for work, under supervision, on assigned topics for higher degrees. (b) Wool Textile Research Council and International Wool Secretariat Scholarships: for work under supervision on problems connected with the processing or the structure and chemical properties of wool fibres or on allied topics. The work is suitable for a higher degree. (c) Wool Textile Research Council and International Wool Secretariat Fellowships: for work under general direction but not necessarily detailed supervision on the physical and/or chemical properties of wool or related topics.

Halls of Residence

The Revis Barber Hall accommodates 200 men students, and the Dennis Bellamy Hall an additional 150 men and 47 women students. They are linked by joint dining and communal rooms, and are situated in their own ground with playing fields only a few minutes walk from the main teaching block.

Tong Hall, on the outskirts of Bradford in 10 acres of ground, retains much of its eighteenth-century character, but extensive modernization provides good accommodation for 50 men students.

Registered lodgings are also available.

Further Information

Inquiries should be addressed to:

The Head of the Department of Textile Industries,
University of Bradford,
Bradford, 7.

Bradford Technical College

Bradford Technical College developed from the Bradford Mechanics' Institute, which was founded in 1877 to provide instruction in weaving and designing for entrants to the textile industry. By 1882 the demand and support of local industries had resulted in the erection of a new building to accommodate departments of Science, Textile Industries, Engineering, Dyeing, and Art. Bradford City Council became associated with the College in 1890, and in 1899 took over full control of the rapidly expanding College. Subsequently, other departments were added, and the Department of Arts became a separate college of arts and craft. To accommodate the Textile Department a new building was opened on Carlton Street in 1911, for which two new wings were completed in 1956. Further buildings were added in 1933 to cope with the expansion.

In 1957 Bradford Technical College was designated as a college of advanced technology. This new status called for a change of name and organization, so the new Bradford Institute of Technology (which became the University of Bradford in 1966) was created to undertake the work of more advanced studies and research, whilst the Bradford Technical College continued to provide for the remaining work.

The situation regarding courses in this and other technical colleges is inevitably somewhat fluid, particularly having regard to the introduction of polytechnics in Lancashire and Yorkshire. The following broad information is correct for 1967.

Two-year General Course in Textiles

This provides a means of entry to a National Certificate course in general textile technology for students who do not possess the normal GCE entrance requirements. The teaching of mathematics, chemistry, and physics is experimental rather than abstract, and wherever possible is related to textiles. The textiles syllabus includes a brief survey of the historical development of the textile industry and a survey of the more important textile fibres—natural and man-made—their sources, properties, and uses. This is followed by the processing (including basic principles) of fibres into yarns, and yarns into fabrics, both woven and knitted. Practical work forms an integral part of the course.

National Diplomas and Certificates and the Associateship of the Textile Institute

Courses have been reorganized to enable students to take advantage of the new schemes brought in by the Joint Committee of the Textile Institute and the Department of Education and Science (these bring a closer relationship between the new National Diploma, National Certificate, and the Textile Institute's Associateship awards).

Bradford Technical College offers both full-time and part-time courses leading to the Ordinary National Diploma or the Ordinary National Certificate and to the possible exemption of the Part I examination for the Associateship of the Textile Institute.

The Ordinary National Diploma course (full-time, two-year) gives the student a thorough grounding in textile technology, applied sciences, and mathematics, and a broad outlook of the textile industry; he should thus have a basis for more advanced study in the field of his choice.

The Ordinary National Certificate is a part-time course of 2 years' duration.

Full-time Day Courses

College Diploma Courses. Three-year courses are offered in yarn manufacture and cloth manufacture. They are designed as an extension to the Ordinary National Diploma with a bias towards specialization in the particular field indicated.

College Certificate Courses. Two-year courses are offered in yarn manufacture and cloth manufacture. They are intended for those students who cannot meet the entrance requirements for the Ordinary National Diploma courses and yet wish to make a thorough study of the subject selected.

College Special Courses. The following special day courses are available:

(a) *Merchants' Course,* involving full-time attendance throughout one session.

(b) *Wool Buyers' and Top Merchants' Course,* involving (i) attendance at the College on 4 half-days a week throughout one session; (ii) 6 half-days a week training within industry.

These courses are designed to help students to obtain a reasonable understanding of the materials and processes in the textile industry.

Other Special Courses

To meet the requirements of industry, various courses can be arranged for students with special needs. They may be on a part-time day or full-time day basis.

The following technician courses are available: woollen and worsted raw materials; woolcombing; worsted spinning; woollen and worsted weaving—designing course; woollen and worsted weaving—weaving and tuning course; woollen and worsted weaving—finishing course; City and Guilds of London Institute Full Technological Certificate.

The following craft courses are available: raw materials; worsted spinning; woollen and worsted weaving and tuning; textile mill mechanics' course.

Courses in Preparation for the Associateship of the Textile Institute

Facilities are available for students to study on a part-time day or evening basis for the Associateship of the Textile Institute.

Instructor Training Courses

Instructor training courses are run for the Wool, Jute, and Flax Industry Training Board, and also half-day courses for management personnel, to give them an appreciation of the methods used in the instructor training courses.

Further Information

Inquiries should be addressed to:

> Head of the Department of Textiles,
> Bradford Technical College,
> Great Horton Road,
> Bradford, 7.

Note

The Textile Department and the Regional College of Art collaborate in running a combined course for textile designers leading to the Bradford Diploma in Woven Design. Students are trained in the essential requirements of this profession in the fields of both art and technology.

North-east Lancashire Textile Department
(Burnley, Nelson, Colne)

The Department is a joint organization covering the Municipal College, Burnley, and Nelson and Colne College of Further Education.

The types of courses offered by the Department come under the following headings: general course in textiles; National Certificate course; technician course in weaving.

Specialist Intensive Courses—short intensive courses, lasting from about 1 to 3 weeks, on modern machinery and accessories.

Instructor Training Courses—for instructors in industry run in conjunction with the Wool, Jute and Flax Industry Training Board.

Other Short Courses

Three short courses introduced in 1967 serve as examples of some ways in which the Department serves industry.

Management Personnel. This is intended to provide management with an appreciation of the work of their technicians. It is on the lines of a condensed intensive training scheme, requiring attendance for 4 days, and deals with selected mechanisms on looms and on winding machines.

General Office Personnel. A short course providing a "not-too-technical" approach to trade calculations, including an introduction to metric methods and an appreciation of the manufacturing processes.

Cloth Examination Personnel. A short course on such topics as yarn faults, fabric faults, grading, and handling.

Further Information

Inquiries should be addressed to:

> Head of Department,
> North-east Lancashire Textile Department,
> Municipal College,
> Burnley.

Derby and District College of Technology

The main teaching interests of the Textile Department are directed to Associate of the Textile Institute courses, in which all branches at Part II level are offered with the exception of spinning and design. Woollen and worsted subjects are not offered as a general rule; but there are strong interests in wool, particularly on the research side. The Department has some sophisticated equipment, including an Instron tensile testing machine, which can cope with a variety of material from single fibres to car safety-belts under an exceptionally wide range of testing conditions. There is also a high resolution electron microscope for research on the fine structure of fibres, including wool. The work on wool is carried out under the auspices of the University of Leeds.

Part-time Courses

General course in textiles; Ordinary National Certificate in textiles; weaving; dry cleaning technology; principles of laundering; knitting; dyeing, finishing and printing; College Diploma in technological textile design; analysis and testing of textile materials; Textile Institute and Clothing Institute Associateship courses.

Further Information

Inquiries should be addressed to:

> Head of the Textiles Department,
> Derby and District College of Technology,
> Kedleston Road,
> Derby.

Dewsbury and Batley Technical and Art College

This well-equipped college provides the following textile courses for those living in the area covered by Dewsbury, Batley, Spenborough, Mirfield, Heckmondwike, Morley, and Ossett. In addition, the full-time courses are open to students from all over the world. Amongst several scholarships are those made available by the Heavy Woollen District Manufacturers and the International Wool Secretariat.

The courses are arranged flexibly to suit the varying ability of students and the different needs of industry; they progress from an initial broad treatment of general textile technology to specialization at a later stage.

Full-time Induction Course in Textiles (College Certificate)

A 1-year course leading to the sandwich course (see below). The curriculum includes the theory and practice of yarn manufacture, weaving, designing, and cloth finishing, together with textile materials and general studies.

Sandwich Course in Textiles

Students taking this course, arranged in co-operation with local industry, spend half the year at the College and the other half in industry gaining practical experience. The subjects of the induction course are taken to a more advanced stage, and further specialized studies are added leading to the examinations of both City and Guilds and Part I of the ATI. Successful students are awarded a Diploma in Textile Technology, and are granted Licentiateship of the Textile Institute (LTI) on reaching the age of 23.

Part-time Courses

General Course in Textiles. A preparatory course for students who show promise of being able to take a further course leading to Ordinary National Certificate or a technician course.

Craft Courses (for City and Guilds certificates).

Wool Textile Raw Materials. A 3-year course meeting the needs of wool sorters, sample room personnel, and others requiring a basic knowledge of the raw materials used in the industry.

Woollen Yarn Manufacture. A 2-year course designed to give a sound practical knowledge of woollen yarn manufacture.

Worsted Spinning. A 2-year course for those requiring the technical knowledge to equip them initially for positions as worsted spinning overlookers.

Weaving and Tuning. A 3-year course for those wishing initially to become apprentice loom tuners.

Technician Courses

(a) *Woollen Yarn Manufacture*, (b) *Woollen and Worsted Weaving and Designing.* These two courses, both of 5 years, provide progressive education for technical men wishing to become foremen, and lead to a Full Technological Certificate.

Associateship of the Textile Institute

A complete course in general textile technology in preparation for ATI Parts I and II examinations.

Other Courses

Special courses are arranged on many subjects such as: short refresher courses on various topics for executives, managers, supervisors, foremen, and instructors; Wool, Jute, and Flax Industry Training Board instructor courses; an appreciation of yarn manufacture and its problems (for those engaged in weaving, design and cloth finishing); an appreciation of fabric manufacture and cloth finishing (for those engaged in the raw materials and spinning sections of the industry); chemistry as applied to the textile industries.

Courses are also offered in: textile raw materials; shoddy and mungo manufacture; yarn manufacture; loom tuning; dyeing of textiles; cloth mending and fine drawing; carpet manufacture; textile testing; industrial organization (textiles); and mill engineering and services.

Further Information

Inquiries should be addressed to:

Head of Department of Textiles,
Dewsbury and Batley Technical and Art College,
Halifax Road,
Dewsbury.

Dundee College of Technology

The Department of Textile Manufacture is mainly concerned with the technology of jute and other hard fibres, but this situation is (1967) changing fairly rapidly with the introduction of polyolefines. Amongst the full-time courses there is:

Diploma of Dundee College of Technology in Textiles

The 3-year course covers the study of the fundamental principles of yarn and cloth manufacture, and the practical application of those principles, together with a study of the necessary textile science, mathematics, management, and engineering subjects.

Students satisfactorily completing the course can be considered for the award of Licentiateship of the Textile Institute (LTI); further studies can lead to the Associateship of the Textile Institute.

Further Information

Inquiries should be addressed to:

> Head of the Department of Textile Manufacture,
> Dundee College of Technology,
> Bell Street,
> Dundee.

Lauder Technical College (Dunfermline)

The Department of Textiles provides courses which are designed to meet the needs of those engaged in the local textile industry—the weaving of linen, silk, and man-made fibres, and for the machine sewing of the finished cloth and other fabrics.

Further Information

Inquiries should be addressed to:

> Head of the Department of Textiles,
> Lauder Technical College,
> Dunfermline.

Scottish Woollen Technical College (Galashiels)

This College, which offers a wide range of part- and full-time courses in textiles, is administered as a Scottish Central Institution for Education in Textile Design and Technology under the guidance and authority of the Scottish Education Department. The new building erected in 1964 provides the most modern facilities and equipment for teaching, study, and recreation. At the time of writing (1967) there is hostel accommodation for 16 students, but the new Hall of Residence projected for completion in October 1968, will accommodate 120 students. There is also a College Industrial Training Unit in the form of a fully equipped woollen mill; this provides a close link with the Wool Industries Research Association whose Member Services Unit—Scotland is housed in the same building.

Although the emphasis is on wool processing, both the technology and the design departments embrace the other animal fibres, silk, cotton, flax, and the man-made fibres. Design is regarded as an equal partner of technology, this outlook finding expression in all the appropriate courses. In his first 2 years the design student spends half of his time in the Technology Department studying the properties of fibres and the processes of the textile industry. The main speciality is woven design, but printed and knitting design are included in the courses.

Knowledge of business management is regarded as the third essential in the student's preparation for the modern textile industry. This is provided by the Department of Management Studies in which specialist members of the staff give instruction in: computor methods; industrial psychology; management accounting; production management; and marketing. Additionally the Department provides a service to industrially based personnel by means of an annual residential management conference, top management seminars, senior management study groups based on Galashiels and Aberdeen, a personnel and training officers study group based on Galashiels, and special short courses on computer techniques.

An Elliott 903B computer installation is currently used in courses concerned with the application of computer technology to technological and managerial problems.

The College is actively conducting research in a wide field of subjects covering marketing, chemistry, dyeing, yarn manufacture, design, training techniques, and integrated data processing.

Courses in Textile Technology

A 4-year course leading to B.Sc. (Hons.) deals with the science, materials, and processes of the textile industry at an appropriate level. In his fourth year each student may specialize in either yarn and fabric production, or dyeing and finishing, and he undertakes research in his selected field. Throughout the 4 years, instruction is given in business studies, information services, and certain liberal subjects.

A 3-year course leading to the College Diploma provides instruction in the basic science, materials, and processes of the textile industry, and the application of scientific method and understanding. As in the B.Sc. course, instruction is given in business studies, information services, and certain liberal subjects. In his third year each student may specialize in either yarn and fabric production or dyeing and finishing, much of his time being spent on practical work.

Course in Textile Design

A 4-year honours associateship course gives students the opportunity of attaining the highest standards as creative designers. The successful graduate will be technically competent, and will have developed an aesthetic awareness; in addition he will be conversant with current design-thinking and fully trained in production methods. Instruction is also given in business studies and the other topics mentioned in the above courses.

College Certificate Course in Textile Manufacture

This is a 2-year course providing an introduction to textile processing, the emphasis being on woollen and worsted. Most of the students follow this course with further full-time study leading to examinations of the following bodies: (a) the City and Guilds of London Institute (one of the full technological certificates); (b) the Textile Institute (Part I of the Associate examinations); (c) the Institute of Cost and Works Accountants; (d) the Institute of Work Study Practitioners.

Courses in Management

A full-time course for middle management, leading to the College's Certificate in Industrial Engineering and Management, is designed for mature people sponsored by their employers. The course, requiring 12 weeks full-time attendance, is in three stages spread over four academic terms. Stage 1 covers basic subject matter essential to a satisfactory understanding of management activity involving the study of business economics, accountancy, industrial and social psychology, and statistical method. Stage 2 covers the major techniques of industrial engineering, including applied statistics, management accounting, industrial engineering, personnel administration, and marketing. Stage 3 is concerned with modern management practices and seeks to improve the analytical, questioning, and decision-making skills of the individual.

A 2-year part-time course, leading to the Certificate in Business Administration, is intended for those wishing to acquire a basic education in management concepts and techniques. The subjects studied are: financial administration; business systems; business administration; business operations.

Other courses in management studies lead to awards of the following organizations:

(1) The Institute of Work Study Practitioners (Graduate Examination; Work Study and Industrial Engineering Diploma).
(2) The City and Guilds of London Institute (Certificate in Work Study).
(3) The Institute of Cost and Works Accountants (Associateship Examinations).
(4) National Examinations Board in Supervisory Studies (Certificate in Supervisory Studies).

Block Release

A change-over from day release to block release was made in September 1967 enabling the College to provide for mill-based students from all over Scotland.

Further Information

Inquiries should be addressed to:

> The Principal,
> Scottish Woollen Technical College,
> Galashiels.

Galashiels College of Further Education

The College, which has its own Board of Management and is financially accountable to the Selkirkshire Education Committee, draws its students from the Borders, from Peebles eastwards, and within the watershed of the Tweed basin.

In the 1966–7 syllabus there were three textile courses for City and Guilds examinations, the subjects covered being as indicated below.

Designers' Course

General textile studies. Textile raw materials. Weaving processes and cloth structure and analysis. Calculations. Weaving mechanisms. Textile testing. Cloth finishing. Industrial organization.

Weaving and Tuning Course

This course covers much of the same ground as the above, as appropriate for the different type of student, and includes also workshop practice and mill engineering.

Cloth Finishers' Course

This course covers the same basic textile education as the above two, as required by the student of this particular subject, and includes also chemistry, dyeing of wool and associated fibres, and cloth finishing.

Further Information

Inquiries should be addressed to:

> The Principal,
> Galashiels College of Further Education,
> Galashiels,
> Selkirkshire.

University of Strathclyde (Glasgow)

In the Department of Fibre Science there is a choice of three courses, depending on the entrance qualifications and the preference of the student. Those following the 4-year course leading to a degree with honours in fibre science are given a basic training in mathematics, physics, and chemistry during the first 2 years, followed by courses on the fundamental principles involved in the production of fibres and their processing into fabrics. Students obtaining an honours degree are automatically exempt from the examinations for the Associateship of the Textile Institute.

At the end of the first year of the degree course a student may opt or be advised to take an ordinary degree course in fibre science (3 years in all), in either the physics or chemistry branch. The lecture commitments are less than those for the honours course and the subject is studied to a less advanced stage than is required for honours.

A 2-year course leading to a Certificate in Textile Technology is available for students with lower entry qualifications; it is designed to enable them to pass the Part I examination for ATI.

Facilities are available for students undertaking research for higher degrees such as M.Sc. or Ph.D. The main fields of research in the postgraduate research school are fibre physics, fibre chemistry, and the evaluation and development of textile fabrics.

In fibre physics, research is concentrated on the structure and rheological properties of fibres. The projects may be either fundamental to gain an understanding of the basic relationships between fine structure and physical properties, or applied to a specific end use.

Research in fibre chemistry is mainly concerned with man-made fibres.

Fabric evaluation is carried out in laboratories with controlled conditions of temperature and humidity, climatic chambers, and with special equipment, e.g. for evaluating size-distribution on carpets and thermal conductivity and air permeability of fabrics.

Equipment includes a range of flat and circular knitting machines, weaving machines, and high-speed electronic yarn tension recorders.

Accommodation

There are three halls of residence. Baird Hall for men is located near the University. Mellanby Hall and Lochview Hall for women are both situated in pleasant residential districts.

Further Information

Inquiries should be addressed to:

> Head of Department of Fibre Science,
> University of Strathclyde,
> George Street,
> Glasgow, C.1.

The Percival Whitley College of Further Education (Halifax)

City and Guilds Examinations

The following three courses offered by the Textile Department prepare students for the City and Guilds examinations: (a) technician course in worsted spinning; (b) technician course in woollen and worsted weaving; (c) craft course in worsted spinning.

Instructor Courses

Courses are run as part of the programme for the training of instructors of the Wool, Jute, and Flax Industry Training Board.

Other Courses

Specialist classes in carpet manufacture and in testing for laboratory assistants are run as required.

Further Information

Inquiries should be addressed to:

> Head of the Textile Department,
> The Percival Whitley College of Further Education,
> Francis Street,
> Halifax.

Henderson Technical School (Hawick)

The classes arranged at this further education centre provide a progressive course (part of which may be taken in day-continuation classes) in the technology of hosiery manufacture. The full course, which extends over three sessions, enables students requiring more advanced study to proceed to the City and Guilds examinations. They may then remain at the centre to qualify for the award of the Full Technological Certificate in the manufacture of hosiery and knitted goods. Alternatively, having completed the course at Hawick, they may go on to the Nottingham or Leicester Regional College of Technology and qualify there.

The Hawick Hosiery Manufacturers' Association issues certificates to successful candidates in the Association's examinations in the theory and practice of hosiery. The certificates are in three grades, and the work of the classes is designed to meet the requirements of the syllabuses of the examinations, which have special reference to local practice.

Day-release and evening-continuation classes in mending, machining, and linking, are provided for girls in the hosiery industry.

Further Information

Inquiries should be addressed to:

> The Headmaster,
> Henderson Technical School,
> Further Education Centre,
> Hawick,
> Roxburghshire.

Huddersfield College of Technology

The College has a long history beginning in 1841 when an association of young working men and voluntary teachers began to hold meetings in the Temperance Coffee House. By 1851 this organization had become the Mechanics' Institution, and in 1879 designs of cloth submitted by its members gained the first silver medal awarded by the City and Guilds of London Institute. The status of Technical College was adopted in 1896.

The Government White Paper on Technological Education (1956) included Huddersfield Technical College for further development for advanced work, and subsequently the College was designated as a regional college. The Ramsden Technical College was therefore established as a separate institution in 1963 to enable Huddersfield College of Technology—now (1967) about to acquire the status of Polytechnic—to shed some of its more elementary work, and thus concentrate on National Certificate and Diploma standard, advanced and final stages of the City and Guilds examinations, and degree courses.

The equipment is comprehensive and of the latest design. There are extensive sheds for woollen yarn manufacture, worsted yarn manufacture, and power-loom weaving for cloth, carpets, and pile fabrics. Fifty hand looms are available for creative design.

Facilities for aesthetic development are provided in a design and colour laboratory. In addition, the laboratories of the Dyeing Department are used for the auxiliary subjects of dyeing and textile chemistry, close collaboration being maintained with this Department, and also with the Department of Business and Management Studies.

The Department of Textile Industries provides courses for three categories of students: (1) technologists, (2) higher technicians, (3) ordinary technician/craftsmen.

(1) *Courses for Technologists*

Diploma in Textile Technology. A 3-year full-time course on raw materials, yarn manufacture, cloth manufacture, and general textile technology. This gives exemption from ATI Part I, and prepares the candidate for Part II.

Diploma in Cloth Manufacture. A 3-year full-time course on all aspects of cloth manufacture, including cloth structure, design and colour, and finishing.

Diploma in Yarn Manufacture. A 2-year full-time course on the principles and practice of yarn manufacture—particularly woollen and worsted yarns.

Ordinary National Diploma. A 2-year course on general textile technology for potential technologists, work study and management trainees, and others requiring a broad technical knowledge of the industry.

Certificate in Textile Technology for Merchants. A 1-year full-time course on the technical aspects of all sections of the trade, fibres, yarns, fabric design construction and production, cloth finishing, and testing.

Special Courses for Technologists. Specialized full-time and part-time courses are arranged to suit individual requirements.

B.A. Honours Degree in Textile Marketing. This course is to be included in the 1968–9 session.

Associateship of the Textile Institute. In addition to the above diploma courses there are well-established and well-defined courses enabling a student to take the Institute's Part I examination in general textile technology, and later the Part II examination in a specialized subject.

(2) *Courses for Higher Technicians*

These courses, normally part time, enable students to gain college diplomas in such subjects as fibre technology, woollen yarn manufacture, worsted yarn manufacture, weaving and tuning, textile testing, colour and design, and cloth finishing.

City and Guilds of London Institute. The higher technician courses enable students to obtain the Full Technological Certificate in such subjects as raw materials for woollen and worsted industries, woollen yarn manufacture, worsted spinning, weaving and designing, weaving and tuning, and cloth finishing.

General Textile Manufacture. Comprises one year in the College and 2 years' study on a sandwich basis.

Licentiateship of the Textile Institute. A technician student who has obtained the City and Guilds Full Technological Certificate or other suitable qualification can be considered for the award of the LTI.

Designers' Course. A 3-year sandwich type of course is available for design students.

(3) *Courses for Ordinary Technician/Craftsmen*

Courses leading to a Departmental Award of Practical Proficiency are available in such subjects as woollen carding and spinning, worsted drawing and spinning, yarn preparation, loom tuning and chain making, cloth finishing processes, and mill and design office routine.

City and Guilds of London Institute. Courses for the City and Guilds craft examinations are available in such subjects as woollen carding and spinning, worsted drawing and spinning, loom mechanisms, and tuning and chain making.

Further Information

Inquiries should be addressed to:

> Head of the Department of Textile Industries,
> Huddersfield College of Technology,
> Huddersfield.

Keighley Technical College

The Department of Textile Industries provides part-time day release and evening courses in the theory and practice of worsted spinning and woollen, worsted, and filament weaving. Allied subjects include natural and synthetic raw materials, wool-combing, industrial administration, and textile engineering.

General Course in Textiles

A 2-year preparatory and diagnostic course for those who show promise of being able to follow a sustained course of study in one of the main streams.

National Certificate Course in Textiles

A 2-year course designed to provide a sound basic education in mathematics, science and general textile technology.

Advanced Courses

Worsted Spinning. This 2-year course enables students to take the City and Guilds final examination in worsted spinning.

Woollen and Worsted Weaving (Designing Course). This 3-year course enables students to take the City and Guilds final examination in woollen and worsted weaving (and designing).

Technician Courses in Textiles

These 6-year courses provide a means of qualification for students who will require the detailed knowledge necessary to equip them for posts of responsibility as overlookers, designers, and departmental managers. The courses lead to the City and Guilds Full Technological Certificate. The two technician courses are: (a) worsted spinning, (b) woollen, worsted and filament weaving (designing course).

Craft Apprentice Courses in Textiles

Craft Certificate Course in Worsted Spinning. A 4-year course providing the technical knowledge necessary for positions as worsted spinning overlookers, and leading to the City and Guilds Worsted Spinning Craft Certificate.

Craft Certificate Course in Weaving and Tuning. A 3-year course for apprentice loom tuners in the wool and rayon textile industries, leading to the City and Guilds Craft Certificate in weaving and tuning.

Other Courses

The following are typical examples of special courses that may be available.

Jacquard Designing. A 1-year course of creative work for designers' assistants engaged in figure designing for Jacquard loom production.

Work Study in Worsted Spinning. A 6-week course (one evening per week) for executives, managers, and work study trainees.

Further Information

Inquiries should be addressed to:

Head of Department of Textile Industries,
Keighley Technical College,
Cavendish Street,
Keighley.

The University of Leeds

The Department of Textile Industries, endowed by the Worshipful Company of Clothworkers of the City of London, was established in 1874 as one of the founder departments of the Yorkshire College of Science. The charter setting up the University of Leeds was granted in 1904. Today the Department of Textile Industries consists of two divisions: the older Wool Division, and the Man-made Fibres Division which came into being with the opening of a new building in June 1956. All students make use of the facilities of both divisions, which are in many respects complementary, but training in general textile technology in the early years of degree schemes is followed by specialized training in one division or the other according to choice. Modern machinery for demonstrating industrial processes for the production of fibres, yarns, and finished fabric, is housed in both of these buildings, which also include a design studio, two large teaching laboratories, many other laboratories and workshops, and a specialized library containing over 10,000 volumes.

Although students are admitted for shorter periods, the normal schemes of study extend over 3 years, and in some over 4 years. The following degrees may be awarded:

1. Bachelor of Science with honours in textile physics.
2. Bachelor of Science with honours in textile chemistry.
3. Bachelor of Science with honours in textile engineering.
4. Bachelor of Science with honours in textile industries.
5. Bachelor of Science in textile industries.
6. Bachelor of Commerce with textile industries as a principal subject; the degree may be awarded with honours.
7. Bachelor of Arts in the school of textile design; the degree may be awarded with honours.
8. Bachelor of Arts in the school of textile management; the degree may be awarded with honours.

Technical Management, Research and Development

The courses recommended for students intending to take up such duties as technical management, research and development within industry, liaison work between research associations and industry, and textile testing and quality control, are those leading to the degrees in 1–5 above.

Commercial Management

The wool textile industry offers considerable scope for commercial as well as technical management, and these two functions are sometimes combined in the responsibilities of one man. The courses leading to the degrees in 6 and 8 above are recommended for those aiming at commercial management.

Textile Designers and Designer Managers

The industry also offers considerable scope for those with artistic ability, provided that they can absorb the skills of textile technology as well—for the designer must appreciate the potentialities and the limitations of the machinery used in fabric production. The course leading to the degree in 7 above is intended for such students.

Postgraduate Diploma in Textile Industries

In addition to these undergraduate schemes there is a course leading to the Postgraduate Diploma in Textile Industries. This is intended for both pure science and technology graduates who may wish to take up a career in the textile industry, as well as for graduates who have been employed for some years and require formal training in modern theory and practice. The lectures are designed to suit individual requirements, and each student prepares a thesis on a research project undertaken by him in the department and supervised by a member of the staff.

Degree of Master of Science (by examination)

Suitably qualified candidates can study for the degree of M.Sc. in fibre science by attending prescribed advanced lecture courses.

Degrees of Master of Philosophy and Doctor of Philosophy

Suitably qualified graduates in textile physics, textile chemistry, textile engineering, and textile industries, may carry out research for the degree of Master of Philosophy or Doctor of Philosophy. Such research degrees open up many opportunities for careers in research associations, universities, and technical colleges, as well as in industrial laboratories.

Higher Degrees by Means of Research at the Wool Industries Research Association

Suitably qualified graduates may proceed to the degree of Master of Philosophy or Doctor of Philosophy of the University after carrying out research in the laboratories of the Wool Industries Research Association, which is situated within a short distance of the University.

The Department of Colour Chemistry and Dyeing

This Department of the University of Leeds was established as a part of the Yorkshire College in 1880 and became one of the foundation departments of the new University of Leeds in 1904.

The student of colour chemistry and dyeing today requires a very broad scientific training, which fits him for a career in almost any branch of chemistry, but particularly in the industries concerned with the manufacture and application of dyes. In addition, careers are open to him in research organizations and educational establishments.

Degree of B.Sc. or B.Sc. Honours

The scheme of study for the honours and the ordinary degree are identical for the first 3 years except that candidates for the honours degree take a course in advanced physical and inorganic chemistry in the third year. Candidates for the ordinary degree are expected to translate into English a passage from French, German, or Russian technical literature. Candidates for the honours degree are expected to translate from two of these languages.

Postgraduate Studies Leading to Higher Degrees

The degree of Doctor of Philosophy may be gained by original research and the submission of a suitable thesis, the minimum period of study required being 2 years. The degree of Master of Science may be achieved either by research and the submission of a thesis or by examination and research, the minimum period of study being one year.

Halls of Residence

There are (1967) four halls of residence for men, accommodating about 900 students, and five for women accommodating about 470.

In addition, there are 430 places in the Henry Price Building, a block of independent study-bedrooms. In this building students cook and clean for themselves, and the University authorities arrange for the cleaning of communal areas. There are also about 250 places in other blocks of flats converted specifically for the use of students.

Further Information

Inquiries should be addressed to:

> The Head of the Department of Textiles,
> (*or* The Head of the Department of Colour Chemistry and
>   Dyeing),
> The University,
> Leeds, 2.

Leeds College of Technology

This regional college (designated in 1962) is recognized by the Clothing Institute as a centre for training leading to their professional examinations; the general clothing technology course covers the syllabus for the Part I examinations.

There is no Textile Department in this college; all the courses in the Department of Clothing Technology are for training students for posts in the various branches of the clothing industry. Textiles, under the title of Knowledge of Materials, is one of the ancillary subjects, and is taught to give the student of clothing manufacture a knowledge of the material he uses.

Further Information

Inquiries should be addressed to:

> Head of the Department of Clothing Technology,
> Leeds College of Technology,
> Calverley Street,
> Leeds, 1.

Leicester Regional College of Technology

The School of Textiles, in which the main emphasis is on knitting principles and practice, and the manufacture of hosiery and knitted goods, offers the following full-time courses.

Ordinary National Diploma Course in Textiles

Designed primarily for students who intend ultimately to take up executive posts in the industry. The 2-year course provides a sound training in the scientific principles of textile technology with a bias towards knitting subjects.

Higher National Diploma Course in Textiles (*Knitting*)

A 2-year course providing an advanced study of the science of knitting together with related subjects.

There is a special 1-year Pre-higher National Diploma course for suitably qualified A-level entrants.

Intensive Course

Designed for those having previous experience in the industry who are at least 19 years of age and have a suitable background of technical education. The main emphasis of this 30-week course is on the various aspects of knitting, but other relevant subjects in the syllabus include: warp knitting—manufacture of fashioned and cut garments; manufacture of fashioned and circular knit stockings and half hose, etc.; pattern cutting and making-up; spinning; weaving; textile testing; raw materials; dyeing and finishing; industrial organization.

Students taking this course sit for the City and Guilds examinations in specified subjects to fulfil examination conditions for the award of a Full Technological Certificate. Students completing the course successfully are awarded the College Certificate in Textiles.

Certificate Course

A 2-year course designed to give a sound training in the principles of knitting, and the manufacture of hosiery and knitted goods and allied subjects. Although the relevant basic scientific background is covered, the subject-matter of the course provides a practical approach to industrial requirements. During the course students are expected to sit for the City and Guilds examinations in the manufacture of hosiery and knitted goods and ancillary subjects.

Other Courses

There is a 2-year textiles and knitwear design course, which is run in conjunction with the Faculty of Fashion/Textiles in the College of Art. This course, suitable for girls leaving school at the age of 16, provides a sound training in general textiles together with a specialized knowledge of knitted fabrics and knitwear design.

The School of Textiles also runs a variety of part-time day and evening courses, particulars of which will be found in the current prospectus.

Further Information

Inquiries should be addressed to:

> The Head of the School of Textiles,
> Leicester Regional College of Technology,
> Leicester.

The University of Manchester Institute of Science and Technology

The corporate body now known as the University of Manchester Institute of Science and Technology became incorporated as the Faculty of Technology in the Victoria University of Manchester shortly after the University received its charter in 1903. Owing to its independent origin the Institute differs from the rest of the University in that, under its charter of 1956, it has its own governing body and is financed directly through the University Grants Committee instead of through the University Chest. In all other respects it is like any other Faculty of the University, the degrees awarded being those of the Victoria University of Manchester.

The Department of Textile Technology offers four undergraduate courses:

(1) *Honours Degree Course in Combined Studies of Textile Technology and Management Sciences*

Designed to equip the student for trainee managership. Subjects studied are mathematics, textile processes, mechanics, management science, and modern languages.

(2) *Honours and Ordinary Courses in Textile Technology*

For students training for the technological and research side of the textile industry. Subjects studied are: (a) First year: physics, mathematics, mechanics, textile processes and products, textile materials and testing, and a modern language—French, German, or Russian. (b) Introduced in second year: electrotechnics, statistical methods, design in textiles, and textile chemistry. (c) Introduced in third year: engineering methods, economic aspects of textile technology, textile physics, textile finishing, and chemical processing.

(3) *Honours Course in Textile Engineering*

For engineering-minded students intending to seek employment in firms engaged in the manufacture of textile machinery. Subjects studied are: textile material and processes, textile testing, mathematics, mechanics, theory of machines, materials science, engineering drawing, structures, strength of materials, electrotechnics, statistical methods, textile physics, management science, and a modern language.

(4) *Combined Honours in Technology with European Studies*

Satisfies the growing need for graduate studies over a broader field than a single technology or science. The course combines textile technology with languages, and the study of European markets, customs and culture; it equips the student for employment by textile firms recruiting graduates on their overseas sales and management staffs.

Postgraduate Courses in Textile Engineering and Textile Physics

The Department of Textile Technology also offers an M.Sc· course with options in textile engineering (covering textile machinery design, advanced electrotechnics, advanced kinematics, control, vibration, friction, lubrication, wear, and research methods, etc.), and in textile physics (covering polymer physics, structure and physical properties of fibres, mechanics of textile yarns and fabrics, etc.). The full length of the course is 1 or 2 years: "broken-time" arrangements are possible in which part of the time is spent in industry or in approved institutions.

Halls of Residence

There are (1967) seventeen halls of residence licensed by the University, together with a student "village" at Owens Park, Fallowfield, which in total provide accommodation for about 2100 men and 775 women.

Further Information

Inquiries should be addressed to:

> The Head of the Department of Textile Technology,
> The University of Manchester Institute of Science and Technology,
> Sackville Street,
> Manchester, 1.

Nottingham Regional College of Technology

The Department of Textiles provides courses on hosiery manufacture, warp knitting, dyeing and finishing, garment manufacture, lace manufacture, spinning, doubling and yarn processing, weaving, textile testing, textile chemistry, and textile physics—the emphasis being on training for the hosiery industry.

There are full-time, day-release, and evening courses. Full-time courses are of two or three years' duration, the middle year of the

3-year sandwich course being spent in industry under the supervision of industrial and college tutors.

Full-time Courses

Ordinary National Diploma in Textile Technology (2-year course).

Higher National Diploma in Textile Technology (2-year course).

College Diploma in Textile Technology (3-year course).

The above three courses provide for the education of technologists and executives for the textile industry, with special emphasis on knitted fabrics and goods.

Higher National Diploma in Applied Chemistry (Dyeing).

College Diploma in Dyeing and Finishing.

The above two courses are designed to produce a sound scientific and technological training for the chemist intending to make a professional career in the dyeing and finishing section of the textile industry. Both of these are 3-year courses.

Professional Courses

Courses are available for students desiring to take the examinations of the Textile Institute, the Society of Dyers and Colourists, and the Clothing Institute.

City and Guilds of London Institute

Day-release and evening courses extending over 4–5 years are arranged in hosiery manufacture, warp knitting, dyeing, garment manufacture, tailors' cutting and tailoring, clothing technology, and wholesale textile distribution.

Design.

Diploma in Art and Design—Fashion/Textiles.

Certificates in Fashion Design and Textile Design.

Schemes are run in conjunction with the College of Art and Design whereby their students in the above courses receive instruction at the College of Technology. Subjects include the properties and uses of raw materials; and the properties, design, and manufacture of knitted fabrics and garments.

Other Courses

Amongst the other courses available are garment manufacture, lace manufacture, sewing machine operators, sewing machine mechanics, clothing engineering technology, warp knitting, hosiery mechanic/engineer's course, seamless hose and half hose mechanics course, and tailoring.

In addition, postgraduate short courses and symposia are held on particular subjects.

Further Information

Inquiries should be addressed to:

> Head of the Department of Textiles,
> Nottingham Regional College of Technology,
> Burton Street,
> Nottingham.

Oldham College of Further Education

A noteworthy feature of this College, the information about which is taken from the Prospectus for 1967–8, is the Higher National Diploma course in mechanical engineering. This is a 3-year course during the second and third years of which the student can specialize in textile engineering.

A wide variety of group courses are offered leading to (a) National Certificate courses, and (b) technician courses in yarn production or weaving. The technician courses lead to the City and Guilds Full Technological Certificate.

Amongst other courses are textile testing (suitable for laboratory assistants in testing laboratories), and a machinery makers' spinning course leading to the City and Guilds Full Technological Certificate in Spinning.

Further Information

Inquiries should be addressed to:

> Head of the Textile Department,
> Oldham College of Further Education,
> Rochdale Road,
> Oldham,
> Lancs.

Paisley College of Technology

In this College there is a Textiles Section in the Department of Mechanical and Production Engineering. Amongst the courses available—full time, part time, or evening basis—are:

Woollen Yarn Manufacture (*City and Guilds Technician's Certificate*)

The syllabus includes raw materials, spinning theory, spinning practical, mechanics, and testing.

Worsted Spinning (*City and Guilds Technician's Certificate*)

The syllabus includes the same subjects as above in worsted.

Associateship of the Textile Institute

The syllabus, laid down by the Textile Institute, includes the following subjects: textile fibres, fibres to yarns, yarns to fabrics, and textile finishing.

Dyeing Technology

The following courses are conducted by the Chemistry Department:

Certificate in Dyeing Technology. This certificate replaces the Higher National Certificate in Applied Chemistry, and is endorsed by the Society of Dyers and Colourists. The subjects include fibre technology, organic chemistry, physical and inorganic chemistry, and dyeing.

Society of Dyers and Colourists

For students who have qualified for the Certificate in Dyeing Technology the College offers a 2-year day-release course in preparation for the examinations of the Society.

The Textile Institute

Preparation for Associateship can be obtained by attending suitable classes offered in applied chemistry (dyeing courses).

City and Guilds of London Institute

In addition to the woollen and worsted courses above, there is a course in textile dyeing catering mainly for two of the branches of dyeing recognized by the Institute: (i) dyeing of cellulose and allied fibres, (ii) dyeing of protein and allied fibres. In each of these there is the Technician's Certificate and Advance Technician's Certificate.

Further Information

Inquiries should be addressed to:

Head of the Textiles Section,
Department of Mechanical and Production Engineering,

or

Head of the Chemistry Department,
Paisley College of Technology,
High Street,
Paisley.

Salford Technical College

Full-time and part-time courses arranged to suit the needs of industry and the students, are provided for the following sections of the textile industry and trade: textile marketing; wholesale and retail distribution; textile production; industrial fabrics and their production; bleaching, dyeing and finishing; knitting; dry cleaning. A special feature of the work of the Department of Textiles is the provision of post-advanced courses in textiles and related subjects.

Full-time Courses

Textiles and Their Distribution. A 1-, 2-, or 3-year course for the College Associateship, and ATI Parts I and II. It provides training for young people intending to embark on a career in the buying and selling of textiles.

Bleaching, Dyeing, and Finishing. A 3-year course for the College Associateship and leading to the Associateship of the Society of Dyers and Colourists.

Higher National Diploma in Textiles (Marketing). A 2-year course in which the subjects studied include raw materials, yarn and fabric manufacture, fabric finishes, textile testing, textile technology, fabrics (including design), marketing, economics, statistics, business law, interpretation of accounts, and business organization.

Wholesale and Retail Textile Distribution. A 1-year course for the City and Guilds examination.

Part-time Day Courses

General Course (Textiles). A 1- or 2-year course designed to prepare students for the senior courses in textiles and to provide entry to an ordinary national certificate or technician's course.

Ordinary National Certificate (Textiles). A 2-year course leading to the Higher National Certificate (Textiles).

Ordinary National Certificate (Endorsement). A 1-year course suitable for management trainees and those preparing for ATI, Part I.

College Certificate (Textiles (Marketing)). (a) A 2-year course, (b) a 4-year course, followed by a year of specialized study, for those aiming at a career of departmental management in textiles marketing or merchanting.

Ordinary National Certificate (Textiles (Marketing)). A 2-year course leading to HNC.

Higher National Certificate (Textiles (Merchant Converting)). A 2-year course suitable for textile buyers, salesmen, and technologists.

Advanced Textile Technology and Testing. A 1- or 2-year course designed to prepare for ATI, Part I.

Technician Courses

Technician courses for City and Guilds certificates are given in spinning, weaving, knitting, narrow fabrics, dyeing of textiles, wholesale textile distribution, retail management, and upholstery.

Other Part-time Courses

In addition, courses are held in clothing manufacture, textile design (woven and printed), dry cleaning, furnishing, and loom overlooking.

Evening Courses

Evening courses are held in practical weaving (loom overlooking), practical spinning, textiles (marketing), Ordinary National Certificate (endorsement), technician course in weaving, advanced textile technology and testing, dry cleaning technology, textile design (woven and printed).

There are also some special short courses on spinning (overlooker), weaving (overlooker), sewing machine (overlooker), and knitting.

Block Release Courses

With the co-operation of merchanting or industrial firms full-time day courses, ranging in length from a few weeks to 6 months, are conducted in textiles and in bleaching, dyeing, and finishing.

Further Information

Inquiries should be addressed to:

> Head of the Department of Textiles,
> Salford Technical College,
> Frederick Road,
> Salford, 6,
> Lancs.

Mid-Gloucestershire Technical College (Stroud)

The courses in the Department of Textiles cover the varied range of textile work carried on in the mid-Gloucestershire area. Students are prepared for the City and Guilds intermediate, final, and full technological certificates, and for the national certificates in textiles and the Associate examinations of the Textile Institute.

A notable feature of the Department is its expanding library; as a part of a county scheme, Stroud specializes in the literature of textiles and plastics.

Part-time Courses

Preliminary Textile Course. A 1-year course catering for new entrants to the industry. The syllabus includes general textiles, textile science, elementary mathematics, and English.

Ordinary National Certificate Course. A 2-year course, the syllabus of which includes general studies as well as general textiles and textile science.

City and Guilds Courses. Amongst the City and Guilds courses are woollen and worsted weaving, woollen and worsted manufacture, and industrial organization.

Associate Examinations of the Textile Institute. Courses in general and specialized textile technology are available for students wishing to prepare for the Part I and Part II examinations.

Additional Courses

The following are examples of other courses that may be available.

Weaving Course. A full-time 12-week course of practical instruction for Dobcross weavers.

Refresher Courses. A recent example of this type of course is a 1-day course on woollen yarn manufacture, consisting of four lectures, that was held (1966) under the general direction of Dr. P. P. Townend, Senior Lecturer in Yarn Manufacture in the Department of Textiles of Leeds University.

Textile Materials and their Properties. This course is provided for tailors, warehousemen, drapers, and others desiring a general knowledge of the subject. The syllabus includes experimental work on the general properties of textile fibres including artificial fibres. The fastness of colours, stain removal, and other similar subjects are covered.

Induction Courses. These are 3-day full-time familiarization courses held at the beginning of the summer and autumn terms, designed for school leavers who have just entered the woollen industry.

Instructor Courses. Short, full-time courses are arranged at intervals as required, in conjunction with the Wool, Jute and Flax Industry Training Board.

Further Information

Inquiries should be addressed to:

> Head of the Department of Textiles,
> Mid-Gloucestershire Technical College,
> Stratford Road,
> Stroud,
> Glos.

West Wiltshire and Trowbridge College of
Further Education

The Department of Textiles provides full-time, block release, and part-time courses.

Full-time Course

Students enrolling for a full-time technical course may specialize in textiles. This course has been designed specially to provide the basic education necessary for intending apprentices.

Block Release Courses

Students may attend full-time for 5 or 6 weeks each term. The course leads to the City and Guilds intermediate examinations in 2 years and to the final examination in 4 years. Students not requiring to take an external examination may attend block release for a shorter period if desired.

Part-time Courses

The part-time day and evening courses cover all branches of the woollen and worsted industries. Courses are offered leading to the City and Guilds final examinations. Intermediate certificates are awarded to students who complete successfully the first 3 years of any particular course and pass the necessary examination. Successful students may then take the final examination at the end of the fifth year. A student having attained the age of 21 years and having passed the final examination, may obtain a Full Technological Certificate in that course by passing the Institute's examination in either industrial organization or raw materials, and in mill engineering and services. He may then apply for Licentiateship of the Textile Institute. In addition, the Department offers a course for Associateship of the Textile Institute to successful students who have completed a full course.

The part-time day and evening classes cover a wide range of subjects including, in addition to the subjects mentioned above: fibre technology and yarn manufacture, wool combing, drawing and spinning, carding and spinning practice, preparatory processes, dyeing of wool and associated fibres, mechanism and tuning, pattern weaving, weaving and preliminary operations theory, weaving machinery theory, cloth finishing, design and cloth analysis, testing, hand loom weaving, and general textile technology.

Other Special Courses

Fibres and Fabrics. This course, arranged in collaboration with the Commerce Department and the Women's Subjects Department, gives the essential background knowledge of fibre qualities and cloth structure required by sales personnel in the ladies' and men's wear, soft furnishings, carpets and other trades. Testing and analysis of fibres and fabrics and practical work in the dyeing of wool and the production of yarns and cloth are included.

Cloths, Clothes and Soft Furnishings. When sufficient numbers are enrolled, a 5-week part-time course is held on drapery; men's, women's, and children's wear; carpets and household furnishings; and knitted goods. The course is intended to illustrate the various types of textiles in general use. It is designed for members of the general public wishing to broaden their knowledge of the different varieties of cloths and knitted fabrics worn, and of carpets and furnishings used in the home.

Operative Training of Weavers Entering the Industry. This 12-week course provides people with the necessary training and the background knowledge of the nature of the work involved before entering the industry as weavers.

Handicraft Weaving. This is a 3-term course of evening classes for those wishing to make fabrics for wearing apparel, table mats, hand bags, tapestries and similar articles.

Further Information

Inquiries should be addressed to:

> Head of the Department of Textile Technology,
> West Wiltshire and Trowbridge College of Further
>   Education,
> College Road,
> Trowbridge.

SOME LITERATURE ON CAREERS AND EDUCATION

DENT, H. C. (Ed.), *The Year Book of Technical Education and Careers in Industry*, Adam & Charles Black. Information is given on universities and technical colleges, examining bodies, research associations, and other industrial institutions.

SHIMMIN, A. N. (Professor of Social Science), *The University of Leeds—the first half-century*, published for the University of Leeds at the University Press, Cambridge, 1954. The author of this history was Pro-Vice-Chancellor 1951–3.

WHEATLEY, D. E. (Ed.), *Industry and Careers—a study of British industries and the opportunities they offer*, Iliffe, 1961. In addition to such general sections as planning a career and opportunities for women in industry, there are sections on the wool textile industry, other natural fibres, the hosiery industry, the textile dyeing and finishing industry, the clothing industry, and on textiles other than wool.

Careers and Education, the Textile Institute, Manchester, 1966. This booklet gives much invaluable information, conveniently collected together, on textile education. There are sections on opportunities, salaries, overseas opportunities, courses in textiles, entrance qualifications, the Textile Institute, scholarships, addresses of textile organizations, universities and colleges offering courses in textiles with details of some of the courses.

Careers in the Industrial Research Associations, produced by the Committee of Directors of Research Associations, 24 Buckingham Gate, London, S.W.1. (see p. 116).

A Compendium of Advanced Courses in Technical Colleges, published by the Regional Advisory Councils in England and Wales.

Further Education for School Leavers, prepared by the Ministry of Education and the Central Office of Information.

Choice of Careers, HMSO. Amongst the textile and kindred industries this series of booklets includes: *Wool Textiles and Carpets; Hosiery, Knitwear and Lace; Clothing Manufacture; Bespoke Tailoring; Laundry and Dry-Cleaning; Silk, Rayon, Nylon, and Cotton Cloth Manufacture.*

Degree and Higher National Diploma Courses in Technical Colleges, prepared by the Department of Education and Science. An official guide to the colleges and courses covered by the new Information and Advisory Service.

On Course, Department of Education and Science. A quarterly journal of education for industry and commerce.

International Wool Secretariat, Department of Education and Training (see p. 103).

CHAPTER 2

The Principal Organizations Within The Wool Textile Industry

CENTRAL ORGANIZATIONS

The three central representative organizations in the wool textile industry are the Wool Textile Delegation, the Wool (and Allied) Textile Employers' Council, and the National Wool Textile Export Corporation. They are affiliated to the Confederation of British Industry. In addition to their normal everyday activities both the Delegation and the Export Corporation send confidential reports to all member firms every 3 months. These reports (which include the usual annual report) explain in some detail the activities undertaken on behalf of member firms, and also serve as a means of distributing information received from the Confederation of British Industry, government departments, and other organizations. By means of these three bodies, and others referred to below, the industry is closely knit and highly organized at national, regional, and district levels. It is owing to the efforts of all of these organizations and the firms and individuals they represent that the British wool textile industry achieves such satisfactory results in both the home and overseas markets.

Although in 1966 Japan was the largest importer of Australian wool, the British industry is the largest consumer of wool produced in Australia, South Africa, New Zealand, and South America. It also imports mohair from Turkey, South Africa, and Texas; cashmere from China; and camel hair, alpaca, vicuna, rabbit hair, reindeer hair, and other speciality fibres from many sources. Consumption of virgin wool amounted to 388·4 million lb in 1966.

The industry comprises about 1700 firms, of which nearly half are engaged in the export trade; tops (combed wool), hand knitting yarns, and woollen and worsted cloths are sold in more than 160 overseas markets. Britain is, in fact, the world's largest exporter of wool textiles, its exports amounting to more than a quarter of the total world trade in wool textiles. Over the period 1956–66 the industry's export earnings averaged £160m. annually —and this figure would have been much greater but for quotas and prohibitive restrictions in two-thirds of the world's markets, where the sales potential for British wool goods remains very high. In 1966, when direct exports of wool and wool textiles amounted to £151m. (3 per cent lower than in 1965), it was estimated that by exports and import savings the industry contributed £226m. to Britain's balance of payments.

Some idea of the objectives and achievements of the three central organizations is implicit in the above short account. These and some other organizations within the industry will now be considered individually, but space permits only brief remarks on each.

WOOL TEXTILE DELEGATION
Lloyds Bank Chambers, Hustlergate, Bradford, 1

The Delegation, whose structure is shown in Fig. 1 (page 61), comprises the Yorkshire organizations, the Scottish, Northern Ireland, and West of England employers' associations, the Pressed Felt Manufacturers' Association, and the London wool brokers.* It thus represents the interests of the United Kingdom industry in industrial and commercial matters, and notably in relations with government departments, the Confederation of British Industry, and other textile industries both at home and abroad. Firms in the industry are members of the Delegation not directly but through membership of the constituent associations.

---

* In addition, the Dyers' and Finishers' Association and the Woollen Yarn Spinners' Federation have (1968) become members of the Delegation.

WOOL (AND ALLIED) TEXTILE EMPLOYERS' COUNCIL
Lloyds Bank Chambers, Hustlergate, Bradford, 1

The Employers' Council, whose structure is shown in Fig. 2, deals with such matters as wages, working conditions, and productivity in Yorkshire, where 85 per cent of the industry is situated. It is to the credit of the Employers' Council, and that of the National Association of Unions in the Textile Trade (NAUTT—see below) and the General and Municipal Workers' Union (GMWU), that there has (1967) not been a major dispute in the industry for nearly 40 years, and there have been very few minor ones. The Employers' Council is responsible for the Management Services Centre (see below). A recent (1966) example of work in the welfare field is the achievement of an agreement with the NAUTT and GMWU on safety and accident prevention. The agreement recommended the establishment of an Accident Prevention Committee in units employing 150 or more workpeople.

NATIONAL WOOL TEXTILE EXPORT CORPORATION
EXPORT GROUP, NATIONAL WOOL TEXTILE EXECUTIVE
Commerce House, Bradford, 1

These joint organizations promote and protect the trade of some 800 British wool textile exporters. The Export Corporation spends about £200,000 a year on promoting the industry's exports by means of major campaigns in the United States, Canada, South Africa, and western Europe, on participation in exhibitions and British Weeks overseas, and on general promotional work in smaller markets. The Export Group safeguards members' interests in regard to such matters as tariffs, import quotas, trade marks, and unfair trade practices.

The Export Corporation's trade mark, a design showing an interlacing of warp and weft threads within the Union Jack, has been registered in this country as a certification trade mark and regulations governing its use have been approved by the Registrar

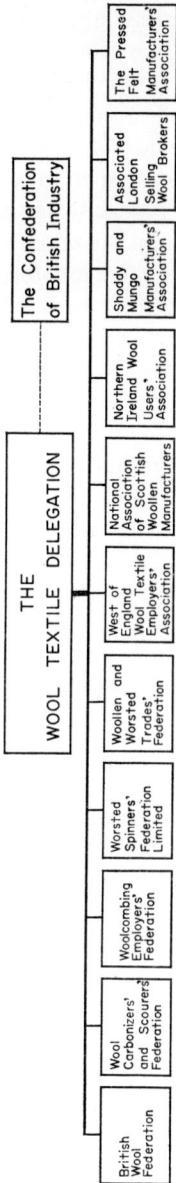

FIG. 1. The Wool Textile Delegation—membership. (By permission.)

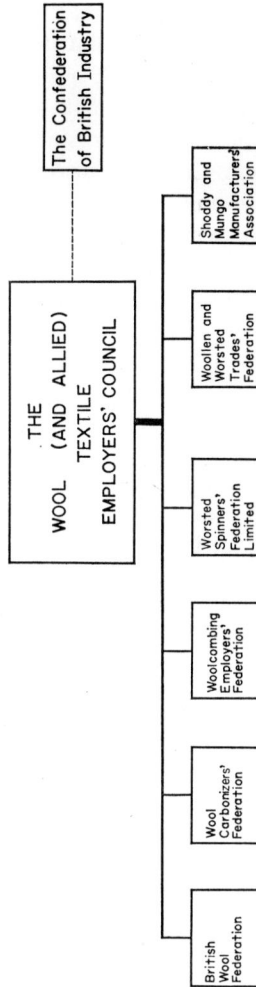

FIG. 2. The Wool (and Allied) Textile Employers' Council. (By permission.)

of Trade Marks. This "Woven in the British Isles" label is promoted in a number of countries throughout the world as an authentic symbol of British origin, guaranteeing to the buyer that cloth so identified has been wholly processed in the United Kingdom. The certification mark can be applied as a sew-in label, a swing ticket, a cloth transfer, or be incorporated in seals attached to cloth lengths; it is proving to be a valuable selling aid to cloth manufacturers and retailers. The formalities required for registering as an authorized user have been reduced to a minimum, and the only cost involved is in the purchase of labels or tickets, which are supplied at a nominal charge.

The work of the Export Corporation is financed by an Export Promotion Levy introduced under the Industrial Organization and Development Act, 1947.

In addition to a yearly report, the Export Corporation supplies its members with quarterly statistical and news bulletins and with a booklet, the *Exporter's Guide to the Wool Textile Markets of the World,* a new edition of or a supplement to which is produced each year. Market reports are also published at intervals as required.

WOOL TEXTILE INDUSTRY CENTRAL PRESS OFFICE
Lloyds Bank Chambers, Hustlergate, Bradford, 1.

Tel. Bradford 25631.

The Central Press Office operates on behalf of the Wool Textile Delegation, the Wool (and Allied) Textile Employers' Council, the National Wool Textile Export Corporation, and the Wool Textile Research Council. It makes effective use of all appropriate sections of the Press and the broadcasting organizations as a rapid and ready means of disseminating information about the industry.

Special news conferences are held from time to time to ventilate subjects of topical importance. One of the most important journalistic events of the year is the Wool Industry Annual Press Luncheon, started in 1962, which is attended by leading representatives of the Press and all sections of the industry. The Press Office arranges regular visits to the industry by British journalists and also by overseas journalists in co-operation with the Foreign Office, Central Office of Information, British National Export Council, and Commonwealth Office.

Editorial material, including illustrated articles on the industry, are supplied to newspapers and magazines in Britain and overseas as supporting publicity for promotional campaigns, British Weeks, etc.

The *Wool Textile Bulletin* is issued every quarter on behalf of the central organizations of the industry and is distributed to the Press, Members of Parliament and of the House of Lords, universities and technical colleges, trade associations, and other interested bodies. The *Bulletin* gives such information as figures of production, exports and employment, and contains articles of topical interest.

BRITISH WOOL FEDERATION
Commerce House, Bradford, 1

The Federation membership comprises wool merchants, topmakers, noil and waste merchants, brokers, agents, fellmongers, scourers and carbonizers, and a miscellany of other firms concerned with the raw material section of the wool textile industry. In addition to the Executive Committee there are eleven sectional committees representing the various interests of members.

The main objects of the Federation are:

1. To promote and protect the interests of the wool trade and to consider and take action upon questions affecting these interests.
2. To represent the wool trade in its relations with such bodies as government departments, controls, other sections of the industry both at home and abroad, railways, shipping, and transport organizations.
3. To collect and make available to members, by means of regular circulars and other methods, statistical and other

information relating to or affecting the raw material section of the trade.

4. To negotiate with trade unions on wages and conditions of employment and to co-operate in dealing with such matters. (This does not apply to the waste section of the industry, in which such matters are dealt with by the General Waste Materials Reclamation Wages Council (Great Britain).)

5. To undertake by arbitration the settlement of disputes arising in the wool trade.

WOOLLEN AND WORSTED TRADES' FEDERATION
Manor Buildings, Manor Row, Bradford, 1

The Federation membership comprises sixteen district associations covering woollen spinners, woollen manufacturers, and worsted manufacturers.

The governing body is a General Council of about forty-five members, and from these certain representatives are sent to the Wool Textile Delegation. In addition, there are sectional committees, such as the Commerce Committee and the Wages Committee.

The main object of the Federation is to promote the interests of the woollen and worsted industry and the trades ancillary thereto.

PRESSED FELT MANUFACTURERS' ASSOCIATION
Royal Liver Chambers, 8 Silver Street, Bury

The main objects of the Association are (a) to secure as far as possible united joint action among its members on all trade questions, and in particular to negotiate with government departments on matters of common interest, (b) to promote, support, or oppose in Parliament or elsewhere any measure affecting the interests and objects of the Association, (c) to promote generally the interests of the members of the Association.

Membership of the Confederation of British Industry, British Standards Institution, Wool Textile Delegation, and other organizations enables the Association to negotiate, co-operate, and communicate at industry level. Similar activities at international level are conducted through the Wool Textile Delegation.

The Association provides for its members a channel for the collection, collation, and dissemination of information supplied and required by them, and distributes information received from such organizations as the Confederation of British Industry, the Board of Trade, and the Wool Textile Delegation. In addition, the Association is a source of information on the pressed felt industry for non-members.

WOOLLEN YARN SPINNERS' FEDERATION

This national body, which at the end of 1967 superseded the Huddersfield and District Yarn Spinners' Association, represents the interests of spinners of woollen and semi-worsted yarns for sale or on commission.

WOOL INDUSTRY BUREAU OF STATISTICS
Lloyds Bank Chambers, Hustlergate, Bradford, 1

Under the auspices of the Wool Textile Delegation, the Wool Industry Bureau of Statistics collects, collates, and publishes statistical material for the benefit of the industry.

The information is distributed to members in a *Monthly Bulletin of Statistics*. An indication of the type of information put out is given by the contents of the *Bulletin*, dated 22 February 1967, relating to the month of December 1966. This includes: United Kingdom imports, exports and re-exports of wool; stocks of wool and wool tops; machinery activity; consumption of wool; production and consumption of tops; deliveries of yarn, cloth, etc.; yearly figures of consumption, production, etc.; changes in production personnel; combing machinery activity; machinery activity—woollen carding sets, worsted spindles, and looms; machinery activity analysis—looms; production of tops and noils; tops drawn in worsted spinning; consumption in woollen spinning, etc.; summary of wool consumption; deliveries of worsted yarn; delivery of woven fabrics and blankets.

WOOL, JUTE, AND FLAX INDUSTRY TRAINING BOARD
55 Well Street, Bradford, 1

The Training Board (under its original title Wool Industry Training Board) was the first board to be established under the Industrial Training Act, 1964. It was established in June 1964. The scope of activities of the Board was subsequently widened to cover the jute, flax, and cordage industries, and so the title of the Board was changed to Wool, Jute, and Flax Industry Training Board in April 1966.

In 1945 the Recruitment, Education, and Training Department of the Wool (and Allied) Textile Employers' Council was formed; this was the first industrial training organization of its kind in the United Kingdom, and when the Wool Industry Training Board was established some of the staff from this department formed the nucleus of the staff of the new Board, which consequently got off to a good start.

All firms in the industries covered by the scope of the Board contribute to the cost of training by means of a statutory levy based on pay roll, but the Board has a fairly wide and varied scheme of training grants which are paid to any firm or establishment using training methods of which the Board approves.

The Board comprises a chairman who is independent of any of the industries coming within the scope of the Board, a deputy chairman, equal numbers of employer and employee representatives from industry, and a number of educational representatives. Board meetings are also attended by assessors from the Ministry of Labour. In its operations the Board is assisted and advised by board, industrial, regional and area committees which are briefly mentioned below.

The three main provisions in the Industrial Training Act are:

(1) To ensure an adequate supply of properly trained men and women at all levels in industry.

(2) To secure an improvement in the quality and efficiency of industrial training.

(3) To share the costs of training more evenly between firms.

Board Committees of the Wool, Jute and Flax Industry Training Board

(a) *Training Committees*—the responsibilities of these are shown in Fig. 3.

(b) *Training Supply Committee*—covers recruitment, advice, and promotion for firms falling within the scope of the Board, and careers advice on behalf of all industries covered by the Board.

(c) *Executive Committee*—covers all matters, together with implementation and supervision of Board decisions, and decides all matters of detail, and deals with urgent matters requiring immediate decisions.

Industrial Committees

These committees provide a forum for discussion of matters relating to Board activities by representatives of each section of the industry, as shown in Fig. 3. Their terms of reference are to advise the Board, and they do not have any executive powers.

Regional and Area Committees

The purpose of these committees is to advise and help the regional and area advisers in their work, and to reflect regional and area opinion. Like the industrial committees, they have no executive powers.

Board Activities

Training courses are held in different parts of the country for the many skills in the industries covered by the Board, including courses for training officers. National conferences are organized for young trainees employed in the industries, the conferences being open to delegates from England, Scotland, and Wales.

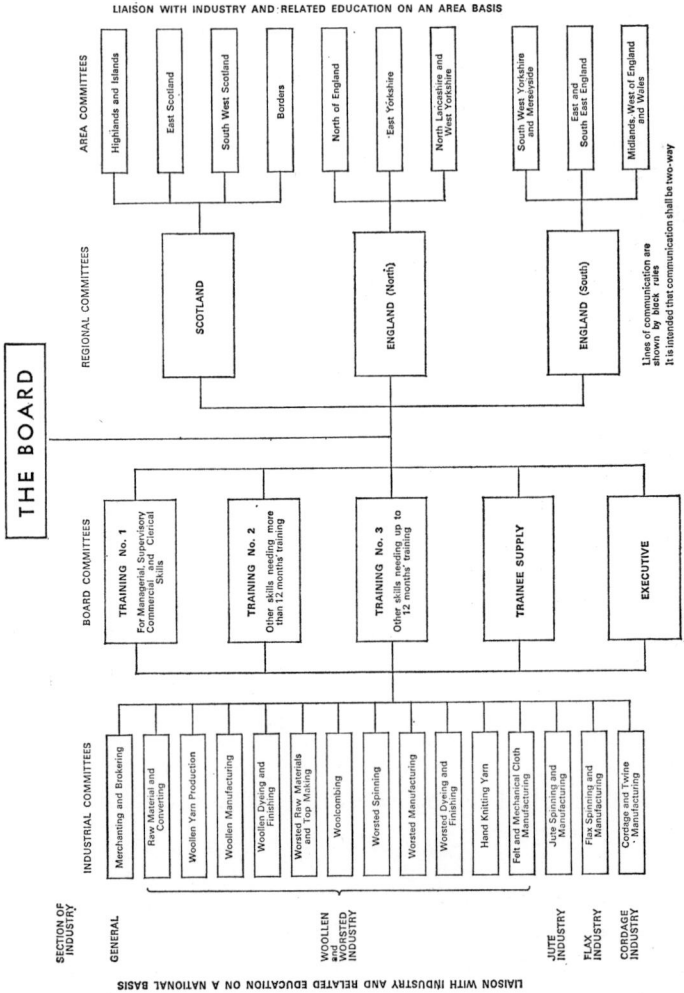

Fig. 3. Wool, Jute, and Flax Industry Training Board—main standing committees. (By permission.)

Recruitment promotion is an important facet of the Board's activities; career prospects are publicized by means of representation at careers conventions, talks at schools, and in many other ways.

These are but a few of the activities of the Board which in its new form is a young organization continually seeking new ways of helping industry to recruit entries and train them in the best possible way.

Scotland

The Scottish Office of the Board is at 15 Alva Street, Edinburgh, 2.

Literature

Industrial Training (Wool Industry Board) Order 1964 No. 907.

Industrial Training Levy (Wool) Order 1965 No. 1158.

Industrial Training (Wool, Jute and Flax Board) Order 1966 No. 428.

Industrial Training Levy (Wool, Jute and Flax) Order 1966 No. 954.

Industrial Training Levy (Wool, Jute and Flax) Order 1967 No. 989.

The above are available from HMSO.

Industrial Training Act 1964—general guide. This pamphlet is available free from the local offices of the Ministry of Labour.

Bulletin. The Board's *Bulletin* is sent to all establishments concerned with the Board's activities, including employers' organizations, trade unions, youth employment offices, colleges of further education, and other organizations connected with education and training in the industries concerned.

MANAGEMENT SERVICES CENTRE
Pierremont, Toller Lane, Bradford, 9

During the Second World War labour shortages stressed the importance of productivity, and with the emergence of new machinery during the early post-war years the industry appreciated the need for applying the techniques of scientific management. In order to promote the greater use of work study and other management aids the Wool (and Allied) Textile Employers' Council set up its own department for the provision of training courses and a consultancy service available to all firms in the industry. This department, which was then known as the Work Study Centre, ran its first course in 1954. The Centre, which is entirely self-supporting, began to undertake increasing amounts of management services work, and so in 1967 it was renamed the Management Services Centre.

By 1967 The Management Services Centre had trained nearly 400 work study officers for firms in the industry; with a full-time staff of twenty-six, courses in various aspects of production management are held, and the consultancy work increases steadily. From the start an important aspect of the Centre's activities has been the follow-up service for those trained at the Centre.

The staff are engaged on assignments in every section of the industry, ranging widely in scope and including labour redeployment, cost analysis studies, management structure and organization, machinery evaluations for re-equipment, production control, and the installation of data processing and computor systems. The service extends over the whole of the United Kingdom, work being done in mills in Scotland, the west of England, and Northern Ireland.

The Centre has always enjoyed good relations with the trade unions, and approval of its work and organization has been given by the wool textile industry's Economic Development Council.

ECONOMIC DEVELOPMENT COMMITTEE FOR
THE WOOL TEXTILE INDUSTRY

National Economic Development Office, Millbank Tower,
21/41 Millbank, London, S.W.1

This Committee (the wool textile industry's "Little Neddy")
was one of the original nine EDCs set up at the beginning of 1964.
It held its first meeting on 25 May 1964, and normally meets every
two months. Most of the meetings are held in Bradford, the remainder at the National Economic Development Office in
London.

The first chairman of the Committee, appointed in 1964, was
Mr. W. H. Mosley Isle, a retired chartered accountant with a life-
long experience of the industry. The members of the Committee
include representatives of employers, employees, and government
departments, and also independents and a representative from the
National Economic Development Office.

The EDCs, of which there were twenty-two in 1967, are voluntary bodies created by the National Economic Development
Council as a formal link to associate industry and its voluntary
organizations with the national objectives agreed by the Council.
Their terms of reference are as follows:

> Within the context of the work of the National Economic Development
> Council and in accordance with such working arrangements as may be
> determined from time to time between the Council and the Committee,
> each Committee will
>
> (i) examine the economic performance, prospects and plans of the indus-
> try and assess from time to time the industry's progress in relation
> to the national growth objectives and provide information and fore-
> casts to the Council on these matters;
> (ii) consider ways of improving the industry's economic performance,
> competitive power and efficiency, and formulate reports and recom-
> mendations on these matters as appropriate.

The work undertaken by the EDC has fallen neatly under the
two headings suggested in the terms of reference. The EDC was,
for example, closely involved in the preparation of the wool
textile section of the National Plan which was published in 1965.

The EDC has also considered several aspects of the industry's economic performance, competitive power and efficiency.

(a) *Marketing*. The EDC has formed a Marketing Study Steering Group to undertake a major study of the marketing of the industry's products and the production processes needed to satisfy market requirements. This study is probably the most important ever undertaken in the industry and the most wide ranging to have been undertaken by an EDC.

(b) *Manpower*. The EDC has set up a working party to study the industry's manpower situation. Currently (1967) the working party is looking into the supply of and demand for labour in the industry, ways of attracting labour and retaining it, and is to undertake a study of ways of improving the use of manpower in order to increase productivity.

(c) *Exports*. The EDC has prepared an analysis of some of the industry's major export markets and has also published two occasional papers on aids to exporters. One describes the facilities offered by the Export Credits Guarantee Department, and the other describes the services to exporters provided by British commercial officers overseas.

(d) *Machinery*. At the instigation of the EDC, joint maker-user committees have been set up with representatives of the Mechanical Engineering EDC to discuss how United Kingdom machinery manufacturers can help to meet more fully the machinery requirements of the wool textile industry. The EDC is also pressing for more detailed information about imports of textile machinery to be given in the Overseas Trade Accounts.

Other topics discussed by the EDC include imports, statistics, qualified personnel, obstacles to efficiency, work study, and the Review of Yorkshire and Humberside.

NATIONAL ASSOCIATION OF UNIONS IN THE TEXTILE TRADE

Unity Chambers, Manningham Lane, Bradford, 1

The NAUTT, which was formed in 1917, comprises eighteen trade unions in the wool textile industry, most of which are craft based. Amongst these are the National Union of Dyers, Bleachers, and Textile Workers (by far the largest, and covers all the non-apprenticed workpeople in the industry), the National Wool-sorters' Society, and the Scottish Council of Textile Trade Unions. Major issues in industrial relations, such as the negotiation of wages, hours, and conditions of employment, are dealt with by the NAUTT, but on all other matters each union has autonomy.

Wages, hours, and conditions of employment are matters for negotiation between the Executive Committee of the NAUTT and the Wool (and Allied) Textile Employers' Council; and, as already remarked in the section on the Employers' Council, it is to the credit of both these organizations that there has (1967) been no major dispute in the wool textile industry for nearly 40 years. The Association also maintains good relations with, and co-operates with, the Management Services Centre (originally known as the Work Study Centre); new incentive wage structures have been established by the Management Services Centre with the full co-operation of the unions concerned. The NAUTT appreciates that the prosperity of its members is bound up with that of the firms for which they work, and that a higher standard of living depends on the efforts of all concerned to produce quality goods at lower costs.

The Association is much concerned with the problem of accidents in the wool textile industry, and its efforts in co-operation with the Employers' Council to reduce accidents have been referred to above.

NATIONAL UNION OF DYERS, BLEACHERS, AND TEXTILE WORKERS
Unity Chambers, Manningham Lane, Bradford, 1

This Union was formed in 1936 as the result of an amalgamation between the National Union of Textile Workers, the Amalgamated Society of Dyers, Finishers and Kindred Trades, and the Operative Bleachers', Dyers' and Finishers' Association. Membership covers the wool textile industry in Yorkshire, the west of England, and Scotland, and the finishing sections of the cotton industry; it also covers the silk, narrow fabrics, flax and hemp, jute, dry cleaning, and many other ancillary industries. There are nearly 60,000 members in six districts comprising more than 100 branches.

The roots of the unions that amalgamated in 1936 go well back into the last century. Today, a reverence for this tradition is blended with an appreciation of the need for keeping up to date, and for many years a professionally trained work study officer has been employed on the Union's staff.

NATIONAL WOOLSORTERS' SOCIETY
40 Little Horton Lane, Bradford, 5

The Society, like the above Union, has a long history, going back to the Bradford Woolsorters' Society which was established in 1838, and the National Union of Woolsorters established in 1889. Today there are branches in Bradford, Shipley, Keighley, Halifax, and Darlington. The Leicester branch, founded in 1903, had to be closed in 1966 owing to the membership having been reduced because of the closure of a local firm; the remaining members were transferred to the Bradford branch.

The Executive Council of the Society holds discussions with the British Wool Federation on such matters as employment and training. The Society is much concerned, for example, that there should be an equable balance between the number of apprentices recruited and the number of sorters employed, and that the best possible type of training should be given to sorters and graders.

SCOTLAND

Scottish organizations are referred to in Chapter 6.

CHAPTER 3

Other Organizations of Importance
to The Wool Textile Industry

THE TEXTILE INSTITUTE
10 Blackfriars Street, Manchester, 3

The Textile Institute is the professional organization for the whole textile industry, and is thus concerned with all the textile fibres. Briefly, its purpose is to advance the general interests of the industry by fostering scientific and technological developments and technical education. It was founded in 1910, granted a Royal Charter in 1925, and a Supplemental Royal Charter in 1955. The major outcome of the latter was that associates and fellows of the Textile Institute received the status of Chartered Textile Technologists. Membership in 1967 amounted to about 7700, including some 2000 overseas members.

Periodical Publications

After several stages of reorganization the monthly issue of literature now comprises three publications: *The Textile Institute and Industry*, *Journal of the Textile Institute*, and *Textile Abstracts*.

The Textile Institute and Industry, introduced in January 1963, contains articles on recent advances in the science and technology of textile fibres, machinery, and processes, written by experts but in language suited to the general membership. It also includes news of general interest to members, summaries of group, section, and Institute meetings and conferences—both at home and abroad, book reviews, an appointments register, advertisements of situations vacant, and much else.

Journal of the Textile Institute, introduced in January 1967, replaces the old transactions section of the *Journal*. It contains papers on original research, reviews of literature, accounts of investigations of a practical nature, and papers giving background information to methods of test.

Textile Abstracts, introduced in March 1967, replaces the abstracts section of the *Journal*. It contains *Wool Abstracts*, provided by the Wool Industries Research Association; other abstracts provided by the relevant research associations are on cotton, silk, and man-made fibres; hosiery; jute; laundering; and hat and felt. There are also abstracts of Japanese vernacular literature and clothing and making-up.

Books published by the Institute

The Institute's books are included in the various lists of literature given later in the present book. Of particular importance in connection with the wool textile industry are *Review of Textile Progress, Mechanics for Textile Students, Textile Terms and Definitions* (see p. 132), *Worsted Drawing and Spinning,* and *Identification of Textile Materials* (see p. 168). A current list of books can be obtained from the Institute.

Education

The Institute sets standards of education, acts jointly with the Department of Education and Science in supervising National Certificates and National Diplomas in Textiles, and awards its own qualifications of Fellowship (FTI), associateship (ATI), and licentiateship (LTI).

For the award of a fellowship, a member or associate must have the necessary qualifications and experience, and by means of a thesis, scientific publications, patents, etc., must satisfy the Diplomas Committee that he has made a substantial contribution to the advancement of knowledge relating to the textile industry.

The associateship examinations are in two parts. Part I requires a broad knowledge of all fibres, all fabrics, and all processes.

Part II requires a candidate to choose a subject from a list of specializations, the syllabuses of which are published. Having passed Part I, and after a compulsory period of 2 years' further

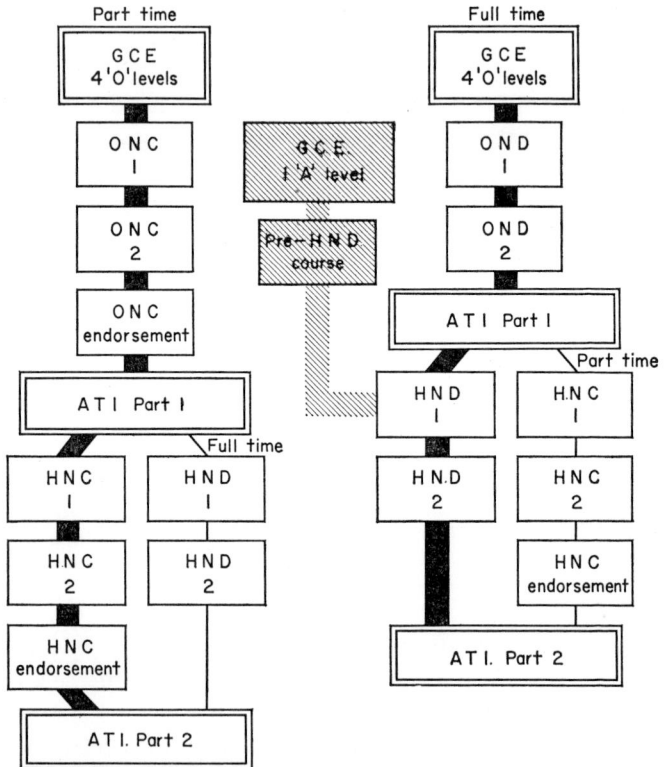

FIG. 4. Chart showing routes to Textile Institute Associateship. (By permission of the Textile Institute.)

training within industry, a candidate may apply to take the Part II examination, but he must be 25 before the ATI can be awarded (Fig. 4).

A candidate for the licentiateship must be 23 or over, should have specialized technical knowledge at an appropriate level in one or more branches of the textile industry, and have a recognized qualification such as a Higher National Certificate.

For further information on the above subject, and in particular for details of relationship between the new National Certificates, the new National Diplomas, and Associateship of the Textile Institute, the reader is referred to the February 1965 issue of *The Textile Institute and Industry*. Information on courses in textiles, qualifications, diplomas, degrees, careers, and similar matters, is given in *Careers and Education*, a special 1966 issue of *The Textile Institute and Industry*.

Methods of Test

One of the responsibilities of the Institute, as laid down in the Royal Charter, is the organization and preparation of standard methods of test for the textile industry. When the need for a new standard arises the matter is considered by various committees; in due course a statement that it is prepared and ready appears in *The Textile Institute and Industry*, and any one interested may have a draft of the tentative method of test. It remains on probation for a while, after which the final specification is forwarded to the British Standards Institution.

TEXTILE SOCIETIES

The Federation of Textile Societies and Kindred Organisations

10 Blackfriars Street, Manchester, 3

The textile societies provide an invaluable forum for discussion and lectures, where management, middle management, and operatives of all types and grades can exchange ideas profitably, and thereby further the interests of their particular district, and often those of the industry as a whole. A complete list of the societies affiliated to the Federation, with the addresses of the Secretaries, is given in *Skinner's Wool Trade Directory of the World*. Amongst these are the societies at Batley, Blackburn, Bradford, Bury,

Colne and Nelson, Coventry, Cumberland and Borders, Derby, Dewsbury, Halifax, Hinckley, Huddersfield, Keighley, Leek, Leicester, Leigh, Mansfield, Morley, Nottingham, Rossendale, Shipley, and Todmorden.

Also affiliated to the Federation are the Textile Teachers Association—Lancashire and Yorkshire Sections.

Bradford Textile Society

Special mention must be made of this Society, the largest of its kind, because of its particular interest and its world-famed *Journal*. The Society was founded in about 1893 by senior lecturers of the then Bradford Technical College; its objects were, and still are, to promote an interest in and a study of the textile industry. Originally the Society was largely concerned with the purely woollen and worsted sections of the industry, but today man-made fibres feature increasingly in the syllabus of lectures.

At the Society's fortnightly meetings throughout the winter months there are lectures on every aspect of textiles from the sheep and its fleece—and the molecular make-up of man-made fibres—to the finished products. In addition to the fortnightly meetings there are four main functions during each winter session: the presidential address, the annual dinner, the annual address, and ladies evening. The speakers at the annual dinner and the annual address are men eminent in their sphere of activities, though not necessarily connected with textiles; in recent years there have been such men as Mr. Edward Heath, Sir Frank Kearton, Sir Paul Chambers, Lord Rochdale, and Lord Netherthorpe (formerly Sir James Turner, President of the National Farmers' Union). The design conferences and the formation of the British Textile Designers' Guild have been referred to on p. 174.

The annual *Journal* is remarkable for its fine presentation; the format, layout, and illustrations, many of them in colour, appropriately point a lesson in design. The articles and reports of lectures and conference papers range from the early history of sheep and of the industry, to the most recent innovations in textile technology. As examples of illustrations, among those in the 1965–6 issue were colour reproductions of paintings by William Blake (The Ancient of Days) and Paul Gaugin (Bretons Collecting Seaweed).

BRADFORD WOOL EXCHANGE

The Bradford Exchange Co. Ltd. was incorporated in 1862, and a 999-year lease was obtained for the site on which the Exchange building now stands. The foundation stone for this building was laid by Lord Palmerston, then First Lord of the Treasury. The Wool Exchange was officially opened in 1867, and ever since then it has been a meeting place where members of the industry do much business, discuss their problems, and—sometimes more important—go to get the feel of the market.

The building was sold to Bradford Corporation in 1964; thereupon a new association was formed, known as the Bradford Wool Exchange, and the main part of the hall of the Exchange continues to serve its traditional purpose, the new association having taken a lease from the Corporation for the management of the Exchange.

The Bradford Wool Exchange Directory and Diary (published yearly by The Bradford Exchange Publications Ltd., Market Street, Bradford, 1) lists members alphabetically with their firms, and firms alphabetically with their members. Information is also given about the council, and such matters as terms of membership and regulations.

CITY OF BRADFORD CONDITIONING HOUSE
Canal Road, Bradford, 2

The Conditioning House was established by a special Act of Parliament passed in 1887 and was opened in 1891 for the purpose of "ascertaining and certifying the true weight, length and condition of articles of the textile trade commonly used in the city".

The word "condition" is used in its technical sense of "moisture content". The need for an authoritative and impartial testing organization arose because wool and other natural fibres readily absorb atmospheric moisture, and this led to serious disputes between buyers and sellers regarding the true weight of consignments.

Tests today are made on raw wool and all other fibres, tops, yarn, pieces of cloth, and garments. Amongst the tests are water, oil, fatty matter, and vegetable matter content; and fibre length, yarn regularity, shrinkage, colour fastness, strength of yarn and cloth, water resistance, wear, moth proofing, twist of yarn, weight per yard of cloth, identification and quantitative estimation of fibres in cloth, number of ends and picks in fabrics, and the causes of faults in yarns and fabrics.

Official certificates are issued giving the results of tests, but no opinions are expressed: the Conditioning House is concerned only with provable facts. The certificates are accepted as legal documents by the Customs authorities of every nation.

The Conditioning House is municipally owned and independent of all commercial interests; its charges are subject to the approval of the Board of Trade. Although the Conditioning House deals principally with the trade, its services are also available to domestic consumers who may be dissatisfied with purchases and wish to have their complaints investigated.

SOCIETY OF DYERS AND COLOURISTS
Dean House, Piccadilly, Bradford, 1

The Society originated in 1884 when a meeting was held on 28 February "to consider the advisability of forming a Society of Textile Colourists". In 1963 the Society was granted a Royal Charter of Incorporation, and the wide scope of its activities may be judged by the objects laid down in the Charter. Amongst these objects are (a) to promote the advancement of technology both in the theory and in the practice of the creation and use of colour and colouring matters, (b) to provide means for the wider dissemination and interchange of knowledge concerning the science and technology of colour and colouring matters including knowledge of application to substrates and of the materials to which they may be applied, (c) to encourage education and research in all or any subjects concerned with the science of colour, (d) to initiate and stimulate research and education in the interests of coloration in all aspects of human life. An important feature of the Charter was the recognition of the status of Associates and Fellows of the Society (ASDC and FSDC).

Education

A Diploma Committee was set up in 1950 (reconstituted in 1952) to prepare an examination system enabling the Society to grant certificates and diplomas; in 1953 "Regulations Governing Admission of Registered Students and the Election of Associates and Fellows of the Society of Dyers and Colourists" were published in the *Journal*, and the first examination for the associateship was held in 1954. In 1958 associateship was accepted as the equivalent of a degree for the purpose of the Burnham Main and Technical Reports.

When the diploma scheme was started there were certain parts of the associateship examination for which no formal course of instruction were available; but the universities and technical colleges co-operated in filling this gap, and wide facilities now exist for those who wish to acquire a theoretical and technological background to their practical experience.

Fastness Tests

Since 1927 the Society has been active in meeting the need for standard methods of testing the fastness properties of dyed materials. The first series of fastness tests, published in 1934, dealt with fastness to light, washing, and perspiration. An improved set of light-fastness standards was issued in 1940, and subsequently these were adopted as British Standard 1006 (Part I): 1942.

Methods for assessing fastness to washing were worked out in collaboration with the British Launderers' Research Association, the work being completed in 1946.

In 1948, at a meeting of the International Organization for Standardization, the United Kingdom and the United States assumed joint responsibility as the secretariat for work on the fastness properties of dyed textiles, and the technical work involved became the responsibility of the Society and the American Association of Textile Chemists and Colorists.

The Colour Index

The first edition of the *Colour Index* was published by the Society in 1924. For the tremendous task of producing a second edition the Society enjoyed the collaboration of the American Association of Textile Chemists and Colorists. Volume I of the second edition was published in 1956 (an appropriate year, being the centenary of the discovery of the first synthetic dye by Sir William Perkin), the remaining three volumes appearing during the subsequent 2 years. The whole work of four volumes is divided into three parts: Part I covers dyes considered in relation to application class, e.g. acid, direct, mordant, subdivided by hue groups; Part II covers chemical structure of dyes and pigments; Part III provides a commercial names index. The first supplement to the second edition was published in 1963.

The Journal

The Journal of the Society of Dyers and Colourists has appeared monthly since November 1884. With the increasing complexity of dyeing theory and practice, some members were finding the more highly scientific papers in the *Journal* difficult to understand. So in 1955 the Publications Committee introduced a series of Explanatory Papers on Modern Theory with the object of easing the problem of communication between scientist and technologist.

There is an abstracts section, which is regarded as an important part of the *Journal*; the abstracts are thoroughly authentic, being prepared by experts in the relevant fields.

Books

Another responsibility of the Publications Committee is to supervise the publication of books that, owing to the specialized subject-matter, might be regarded as uneconomic by the commercial publisher. Examples of these books are: Clayton's *Tables*, 2nd revised edn., 1963; Bird's *Theory and Practice of Wool Dyeing*, 3rd edn., 1963; and Giles's *Laboratory Course in Dyeing*, 1957.

Regional Sections

The following regional sections of the Society were formed in the years indicated: Manchester (1896), West Riding (1897), London (1904), Scottish (1908), Huddersfield (1918), Midlands (1919), Northern Ireland (1946), West of England and South Wales (1959).

In addition there are the following junior sections: Bradford (1898), Leeds (1919), Manchester (1921), Scottish (1957), Leicester (1961), Nottingham (1961).

DYERS' AND FINISHERS' ASSOCIATION
Commerce House, Cheapside, Bradford

The membership of the Association includes commission dyers and/or finishers of wool fibres (and admixtures thereof with other fibres), in their several forms, i.e. loose, slubbing, yarn, and piece goods.

The Association thus differs from many other similar industrial organizations in that the members, as commission processors, do not normally have contact with the eventual end users of the products; their customers are the owners of the materials to be dyed and/or finished.

It is of interest to bear in mind that with the exception of goods exported in the grey state (tops, yarn, and piece goods) the remainder of the products of other sections of the industry are for the most part of little use until they have been dyed and finished. It is the dyeing and finishing that imparts the handle, colour, and general appearance to make the goods saleable. The great majority of fine worsteds are handled by commission dyers and finishers, and a large proportion of woollen goods are dyed on commission for manufacturers who have their own finishing plants.

BRITISH COLOUR COUNCIL
10a Chandos Street, Cavendish Square, London, W.1

The BCC, an independent organization, was set up in 1931 at the request of colour makers and colour users in British industry. Briefly, its work falls into two main categories—colour determination and colour co-ordination. The first concerns the standardization of colours by name and reference pattern of colours in general use. The second concerns the co-ordination of colour in related merchandise.

Each member is entitled to service through one of four divisions: (i) women's wear, (ii) men's wear, (iii) children's wear, (iv) interior decoration; and through one of four sections: (a) wool and knitwear, (b) cotton, (c) silk and man-made fibres, (d) leather.

One of the principal contributions to the wool and knitwear members is in the form and content of the advice given. The Council takes care when recommending colours to the wool textile industry to ensure that they are suitable in every way— technically, commercially, and aesthetically—for a great variety of end uses. Colours are selected or "created" to show the intrinsic qualities of a natural wool to the best advantage; when a new trend is featured for a season, each "wool" colour is seen to harmonize with other materials such as man-made fibres and cotton.

An example of the above is given by the colours for the "Lilac Trend", sent out in advance for autumn and winter 1967. The colours shown on wool fabric were selected to be of the maximum use for tweeds and mixture cloths, and printed wool fabrics, as well as for knitted and woven fabrics. The colours recommended for man-made fibres harmonized with the wool colours but were more suitable for silk and man-made fibres used for light-weight dress cloths, some of which would have been eventually made up into dresses and blouses to wear with suiting and coating cloths of wool.

Similar advice is given in the men's-wear field, in which designers of yarn and cloth for men's suitings are faced with the problem of producing "fashion right" colours dyed in the wool. To meet this difficulty the BCC produces a palette of colours, dyed in slubbing form, 18 months ahead of season. Consultative committees work throughout the year on the specialized work of selecting colours in harmony with these slubbing colours for knitwear and in co-ordinating colours for men's hats (in wool), tie silks, shirtings and leather.

Publications

Dictionary of Colour Standards (see p. 156).

Dictionary of Colours for Interior Decoration, 3 vols., 1949. Volumes 1 and 2 contain colour charts on three surfaces: gloss, matt, and pile fabric. Volume 3 contains an index of over 500 names, cross-referenced with the 378 colours illustrated in vols. 1 and 2, with useful information on the terms used in relation to colour and colour matching.

Colour and Lighting in Factories and Offices, 3rd edn., 1964. A guide to the use of colour and light in industrial and office premises, and to the underlying principles of colour planning.

Machinery Colours Safety Colour Code. A 3-page card illustrating eight colours specially suitable for machinery; and four colours for the *Safety Colour Code*, together with the relevant symbols and details of use. Notes on the use of the colours are included.

Colour Standards for Electrical Cables, Wires, Etc. A swatch showing the fifteen colours from the BCC *Dictionary of Colour Standards* adopted by the GPO for the identification of electrical cables, wires, cords, etc.

The BCC also produces a periodical magazine, *Colour Environmental*.

BRITISH STANDARDS INSTITUTION
British Standard House, 2 Park St., London, W.1

The British Standards Institution is the recognized body for the preparation of national standards in the United Kingdom. The Institution, which dates from 1901, was granted a Royal Charter in 1929, and adopted its present name in 1931 (previously it had been the British Engineering Standards Association). With the transfer of certain functions from the Board of Trade to the Ministry of Technology the latter became the sponsoring department for the BSI.

Briefly, the BSI's main function is to draw up voluntary standards and codes of good practice by agreement among all the interests concerned—manufacturing, using, professional, and distributive—and to promote their adoption.

The BSI is financed by subscriptions from firms, trade associations, local authorities, professional institutions, and other bodies interested in its work, by a government grant, and by the sale of its publications. Its total income in 1965–6 was just over £1,000,000.

Work on textile standards is supervised by the Textile Divisional Council. Proposals for new standards or revisions of existing standards derive to a large extent from the established BSI committees. New projects can be put forward for consideration by any responsible body (such as the Textile Institute), manufacturing firm, or users' organization.

Of textile interest amongst the BSI's Industry Standards Committees are Textile Machinery Industry Standards Committee, and Wool Industry Standards Committee; the majority of the members of the latter are from the Wool Textile Delegation.

International Organization for Standardization (ISO)

The BSI plays a large and active part in the work of the ISO, which was set up in 1947 and is responsible, through technical committees manned by industry and other representatives nominated by the countries interested, for the preparation of international recommendations to be embodied in national standards. The ISO technical committees with which the Textile Division of the BSI is mainly concerned are ISO/TC 38—Textiles, and ISO/TC 72—Textile Machinery and Accessories.

Publications

BS Handbook No. 11: *Methods of Test for Textiles*, rev. edn., 1963. Gives a comprehensive range of procedures for determining the physical and chemical properties and characteristics of textile fibres, yarns, and fabrics. Amendment 1 (ref. PD 5328), published in 1964, and Amendment 2 (ref. PD 5704), published in 1965, are available separately.

SL 33: *Sectional List of British Standards—textile and clothing*, 1966. A 6-page leaflet giving numbers, titles, dates, and prices of standards.

British Standards Yearbook. Contains an index and numerical list of British Standards with a brief summary of the contents of each. A supplement contains lists of the publications of the ISO and other international organizations.

Annual Report. Includes reference to all current work on British Standards and related information on the work of the technical committees of the international standards organizations. It also gives the membership of the principal BSI committees.

BSI News. Issued each month giving details of new and revised British Standards as they are issued, amendments to British Standards, drafts circulated for general comment, new work started, and international recommendations and draft recommendations issued. The main sales office for British Standards and other BSI publications is at Newton House, 101–113, Pentonville Road, London, N.1, but copies may be obtained from the Branch Office at 115 Portland Street, Manchester, 1, where work on textile,

textile machinery, and clothing standards is also carried out. The BSI Library at British Standards House, 2 Park Street, London, W.1, contains, in addition to a full set of British Standards, copies of international recommendations and copies (in the original language) of the standards issued by the national standard bodies of other countries.

PD 4845: *The British Standards Institution: its activities and organization*. A 9-page pamphlet giving a short description of the functions, structure, and methods of working of the BSI, and information on its services.

REGIONAL OFFICES AND INDUSTRIAL LIAISON CENTRES OF THE MINISTRY OF TECHNOLOGY

The Regional Offices of the Ministry of Technology are an integral part of the regional machinery established by the Government to promote more rapid industrial and economic development throughout the country, and to secure a more widespread and vigorous application of science and technology. A major objective is to promote effective co-operation between industry and those independent, academic, and government establishments that are concerned with research, development, and design. The Regional Offices also co-ordinate the work of the Industrial Liaison Centres in their regions.

The Industrial Liaison Centres are located mainly in colleges of technology, a few being in universities; but the Ministry bears the greater part of the cost of operating them. Each centre has one or more industrial liaison officers (ILO), who are members of the college staff and can thus draw on the advisory facilities of the college. They acquaint themselves with useful sources of advice and assistance in their area, and maintain contact with local firms, particularly the smaller ones, with the object of assisting them to make the best use of current technological knowledge and expertise.

The Industrial Liaison Scheme is still being developed, and by the end of 1967 there were about seventy centres in operation, as indicated below.

Yorkshire and Humberside Region

Regional Office—Ministry of Technology Yorkshire and Humberside Regional Office, City House, Leeds, 1.

Industrial Liaison Centres—Doncaster, Huddersfield, Kingston-upon-Hull, Leeds, and Sheffield.

Northern Region

Regional Office—Ministry of Technology Northern Regional Office, Wellbar House, Gallowgate, Newcastle upon Tyne, 1.

Industrial Liaison Centres—Darlington, Middlesbrough, Newcastle, Sunderland, and Workington.

North-west Region

Regional Office—Ministry of Technology North-west Regional Office, Sunley Building, Piccadilly Plaza, Manchester, 1.

Industrial Liaison Centres—Birkenhead, Blackburn, Bolton, Liverpool, Manchester, Oldham, Preston, Stockport, and Wigan.

East Midlands Region

Regional Office—Ministry of Technology East Midlands Regional Office, Cranbrook House, 47 Cranbrook Street, Nottingham.

Industrial Liaison Centres—Derby, Leicester, Northampton, and Nottingham.

West Midlands Region

Regional Office—Ministry of Technology West Midlands Regional Office, Five Ways House, Islington Row, Birmingham, 15.

Industrial Liaison Centres—Birmingham, Coventry, Stoke-on-Trent, Wolverhampton, and Worcester.

South-west Region

Regional Office—Ministry of Technology South-west Regional Office, The Pithay, Bristol, 1.

Industrial Liaison Centres—Bristol, Gloucester, and Plymouth.

South-east and East Anglia Region

Regional Office—Ministry of Technology South-east and East Anglia Regional Office, Abell House, John Islip Street, London, S.W.1.

Industrial Liaison Centres—Chatham, Chelmsford, Hatfield, London (some 12 boroughs), Luton, Norwich, Oxford, Portsmouth, Reading, and Slough.

Scotland

Regional Office—Ministry of Technology Scottish Office, 6 Randolph Crescent, Edinburgh, 3.

Industrial Liaison Centres—Aberdeen, Dundee, Edinburgh, Glasgow, and Paisley.

Wales and Monmouthshire

Regional Office—Ministry of Technology Office for Wales, 69 Park Place, Cardiff.

Industrial Liaison Centres—Cardiff, Newport, Deeside (Flintshire, for North Wales), Swansea, and Treforest.

Northern Ireland

The Department of Industrial and Forensic Science of the Northern Ireland Ministry of Commerce operates a service very similar to that provided by the Industrial Liaison Officers.

Belfast—Technical Information Service, Ministry of Commerce, Department of Industrial and Forensic Science, Verner Street, Belfast.

Literature

> *Regional Offices and Industrial Liaison Centres*, Ministry of Technology, July 1967. This brochure, from which the above information has been extracted by permission of the Controller, Her Majesty's Stationery Office, gives the addresses and telephone numbers of all Regional Offices and Industrial Liaison Centres; it is re-issued periodically.

Technical Services for Industry, Ministry of Technology, 1967. Gives details of the technical information and other services available from Government departments and associated organizations.

Further Information

Inquiries should be addressed to Senior Regional Officers, or to:

Ministry of Technology,
Regional and Industrial Services Branch,
Abell House,
John Islip Street,
London, S.W.1.

OFFICE FOR SCIENTIFIC AND TECHNICAL INFORMATION
State House, High Holborn, Londhn, W.C.1

The principal purpose of OSTI, which is a branch of the Department of Education and Science, is to promote research and development within the area of scientific and technical information and its use—covering new techniques and systems, the improvement of existing information services, and experiments with new services. It assists in co-ordinating the information activities of government and other organizations in this country, and represents the United Kingdom internationally at government level in connection with scientific and technical information problems and activities.

By means of grants and contracts, OSTI encourages research and development that can influence the effectiveness of (i) scientific communications, (ii) classification, storage, retrieval, and translation of information, and (iii) operation of information services for scientists and technologists.

In the field of education, OSTI has three main interests: (a) training for information work, including the provision of suitable training facilities, (b) training for information research,

(c) education in the use of scientific literature and information services.

OSTI's job is to promote—not to provide—information services. As a general rule scientific and technical information should be sought from the many bodies mentioned elsewhere in this book, such as Aslib, other libraries, learned societies, research associations, trade associations, and the regional and industrial liaison offices of the Ministry of Technology. Requests for additional information about OSTI should be sent to the address given at the head of this section.

ASLIB
3 Belgrave Square, London, S.W.1

The name Aslib is derived from the initial letters of the original title of the organization: Association of Special Libraries and Information Bureaux. Aslib is an independent, but government-sponsored, organization whose purpose is to help industry, government agencies, and the academic world, to obtain systematically information on scientific, technical, economic, and other subjects. Its sources of information are world wide and virtually unlimited.

The services of Aslib are restricted to members, amongst whom are manufacturing and marketing companies, government departments, universities, technical institutions, research establishments, learned and professional societies, and public libraries. Inquiries may be made on any subject, and members are either given the information direct or are put in touch with the best sources from which it can be obtained. Copies of journals, reports, pamphlets, and books are located and supplied on loan.

Aslib maintains an index of translations into English of scientific and technical articles that are not otherwise available to the public; in the event of a translation not being recorded in the index the member is introduced to a suitable translator.

Special information groups enable staff working in the same subject field to meet for the exchange of ideas and information and to provide machinery for carrying out specific projects; amongst these groups is the Aslib Textile Group.

Aslib's educational programme is designed to equip the staff of member organizations to make the best use of established practices and new advances in the handling of information; there are introductory, advanced, and special courses. In addition, Aslib arranges meetings and conferences, including an annual residential conference.

Publications

Three periodicals are issued free to member organizations:

Aslib Proceedings: incorporating Aslib information, monthly, contains news of Aslib activities and texts of the more important papers presented at Aslib meetings.

Aslib Book List: a monthly list of recommended scientific and technical books with annotations, lists books published in the English language all of which carry the recommendation of a subject specialist.

Journal of Documentation: devoted to the recording, organization, and dissemination of knowledge, published quarterly.

Aslib also publishes various handbooks and directories.

NATIONAL LENDING LIBRARY FOR SCIENCE AND TECHNOLOGY
Boston Spa, Yorkshire

Originally the need for a scientific and technical library loan service was met by special libraries and the Science Museum Library. Lack of space at the latter library and the growing demand for the loan service led to the position being reviewed by an official committee, and in 1954 the Advisory Council on Scientific Policy recommended that a new national science lending library should be created. The Department of Scientific and Industrial Research (now the Ministry of Technology) became administratively responsible for the new library in 1956.

The main purpose of the NLL is to supplement the internal library resources of existing organizations by providing a rapid loan service for approved borrowers, such as industrial firms, research organizations, universities, colleges, and the larger public libraries. The library does not lend to individuals, but there is a public reading room open to visitors.

The subjects covered by the NLL include the whole field of science and technology. The aim is to maintain literature of value to the practising scientist or technologist, including a comprehensive collection of the recent literature of science and technology in all languages that is, or should be, abstracted. Special features of the library's holdings include a fairly comprehensive collection of (a) the "report literature" issued by the Office of Technical Services in the United States, (b) translations from Russian into English.

The libraries of certain local authorities and technical colleges have direct borrowing facilities; these are listed in the NLL's descriptive brochure.

RURAL INDUSTRIES BUREAU

35 Camp Road, Wimbledon Common, London, S.W.19

The Bureau co-operates with the Wool, Jute, and Flax Industry Training Board in the fostering of training schemes in the Welsh woollen industry (see p. 181). Such work is facilitated by the Bureau's textile designer being based at the area office in Machynlleth in mid-Wales. He pays regular visits to each of the Welsh woollen manufacturers giving assistance and advice over a wide field of subjects. The Bureau is able to assist in advising on colours and designs in fashionable demand for tweeds, flannels, quilts, and other goods, and in many technical matters. Another way in which the Bureau has recently (1967) been helping the Welsh woollen industry is the advising of prospective purchasers of mills that might otherwise be lost to the industry.

Inquiries regarding the work of the Rural Industries Bureau on any of their activities should be sent to the Information and Public Relations Officer at the above address.

COMMONWEALTH SECRETARIAT—COMMODITIES DIVISION

10 Carlton House Terrace, London, S.W.1

At the end of 1966 the Commonwealth Economic Committee was dissolved, and its staff became that of the Commodities Division of the Commonwealth Secretariat.

The Commodities Division correlates data on primary products, raw materials, and certain other goods, and issues the information in several series of publications. Those of interest to the wool textile industry are listed below.

Wool Intelligence (one of the Intelligence Services). Issued monthly, covering raw wool, wool tops, yarns, and piece goods under such headings as: world wool situation; activity in the chief producing countries; activity in the chief consuming countries; activity in other countries; sales and prices; import duties and licensing. Special articles are included on topics of current interest, and there is a Fibres Supplement dealing with mohair, man-made fibres, cotton, jute, and sisal.

Industrial Fibres (one of the Commodity Series). An annual publication presenting in convenient form, reviews of world production, international trade, consumption and prices for groups of related commodities, with special reference to the Commonwealth; included also are Appendixes on marketing policies and legislative measures affecting supply and demand. *Industrial Fibres* covers wool, mohair, cotton, silk, flax, jute, coir, kapok, sisal and other hemps, rayon, and other man-made fibres.

No. 3: *Pakistan*. No. 4: *New Zealand*. No. 6: *Australia*. No. 7. *India* (in the Commonwealth Development and its Financing Series). This series takes the form of studies of the state of affairs in each country. A short introduction pinpoints some of the most important matters, and this is followed by a brief description of the country's recent economic progress and the growth of its labour force, production, trade, national income and capital formation.

World Trade in Wool and Wool Textiles, 1952–63. This is one of the other many books published by the Commonwealth Secretariat, a list of which is obtainable from the above address.

INTERNATIONAL WOOL TEXTILE ORGANISATION
Commerce House, Cheapside, Bradford, 1

The IWTO is an association of organizations interested in the merchandising, processing, spinning, and weaving of wool and allied fibres under private enterprise. Its objects, as laid down in the statutes, are: (a) To maintain a permanent connection between the wool textile organizations of the member countries. (b) To represent the wool textile trade and industry in all branches of economic activity. (c) To promote, support, or oppose measures affecting the trade and industry. (d) To promote the study and solution of economic and commercial questions affecting the aforesaid interests. (e) To ensure the functioning of the International Arbitration Agreement in the wool textile trade and industry. (f) To collect and disseminate statistical and other information of interest to the trade and industry. (g) Generally to do all such lawful things as may be conducive to the attainment of any of the above objects.

The IWTO started as a result of an interchange of visits during the early 1920s between the Bradford Chamber of Commerce and the Chambers of Commerce of Roubaix and Tourcoing. At this time there were quite a lot of commercial disputes about wool, and means of solving them were discussed. In September 1924 an agreement between the above chambers of commerce was signed to the effect that these disputes ought to be settled by arbitration, and that the arbitrations should take place in the country of the seller. During 1925 and 1926, meetings were held in Belgium, Berlin, and Turin at which the organizations representing the wool textile industry agreed to participate in the agreement. At

Turin it was suggested that the talks should be widened to embrace all the problems of the wool textile industry, and thus the work of the IWTO grew. It was agreed that meetings which had been called and conducted *ad hoc* should be given a more permanent form, and the IWTO was formally set up by the adoption of the statutes at a conference in Bradford in 1929.

The initiative for forming the IWTO was taken by the Bradford Chamber of Commerce, but as the list of subjects discussed grew, the Chamber was joined by other organizations. British organizations participating in the British National Committee of the IWTO are now (1967): the Association of Exporters of Raw Materials and Yarns (Bradford); Bradford Chamber of Commerce (Inc.); British Wool Federation; Export Group, National Wool Textile Executive; Woolcombing Employers' Federation; Woollen and Worsted Trades' Federation; Worsted Spinners' Federation Ltd.

Member Countries comprise: Argentina, Australia, Austria, Belgium, Canada, Denmark, Finland, France, Germany, India, Ireland, Israel, Italy, Japan, Mexico, Netherlands, Norway, Portugal, South Africa, Spain, Sweden, Switzerland, United Kingdom, United States, Uruguay.

An essential condition of membership of IWTO is adherence to the International Wool Arbitration Agreement. The following agreements have also been reached: Code of Fair Trading; Standards of Regain; International Trade Agreement Applicable to Imports and to Transactions in Raw Wool; International Agreement Applicable to Transactions in Tops, Noils, Washed and Carbonized Wools, and Wool Wastes; International Trade Agreement Applicable to Contracts in Worsted Yarns; International Trade Agreement Applicable to Contracts in Woollen Yarns; International Contract for Wool Cloth; Wool Labelling.

Much valuable work is done by the committees and subcommittees of IWTO, some of which leads to the publication of test and other specifications. A few of the subjects that have been dealt with during the last few years are: chemical methods for the determination of the composition of wool, core testing of raw wool, sampling of fibres, determination of vegetable matter in wool tops, fibre diameter and length measurement, determination of regain, determination of fatty matter, peroxide bleaching of wool, mothproofing and testing methods, testing of shrink resist processes, and many more scientific and technical inquiries. Other types of subject are discussed by such committees as the Statistics Committee and the Marketing and Information Committee.

INTERNATIONAL WOOL SECRETARIAT
Wool House, Carlton Gardens, London, S.W.1

The IWS was established in 1937 to develop the use and usefulness of wool throughout the world by means of research and promotion. It is financed by the wool growers of Australia, New Zealand, and South Africa, through statutory levies on the sale of their wool, and has branches in nineteen countries. The World and European headquarters are at Wool House, as also is the United Kingdom branch. Retail co-operation in such matters as local advertising, promotion, and display may be facilitated by contacting one of the IWS regional officers resident in the following districts: Edinburgh (for Scotland); Dublin (for Ireland); Bradford (for Yorkshire and Tyne–Tees); Manchester (for Lancashire, North Wales, and West Midlands); and Bristol (for the South-west and South Wales). The regional officers for East Anglia, East Midlands, and the East Coast, and for London West End and the South-east are stationed at Wool House.

The Woolmark

The well-known Woolmark symbol (Fig. 5) is to be a certification trade mark in the United Kingdom which will mean that products so labelled are made from pure new wool cloth or yarn with a maximum tolerance of 5 per cent for non-wool fibres included for visible decoration and $0 \cdot 3$ per cent for inadvertent impurities. The Woolmark is the property of IWS Nominee Co. Ltd. The symbol, which was introduced in the autumn of 1964, is

international and has the same significance everywhere. The pure
new wool standard applies to all forms of merchandise covered by
the symbol, but there are additional standards of tensile strength
for garments made from woven worsted cloths, and of colour
fastness to light and water for hand knitting wools and woven
and machine knitted woollen and worsted fabrics used in garments. The promotion of the Woolmark symbol is a flexible and
growing campaign, additional performance characteristics such as

Certification Trade Mark applied for
PURE NEW
wool

FIG. 5. The Woolmark—certification trade mark. (By permission of
the International Wool Secretariat.)

shrink resistance for knitwear being specified as time goes on.
Information regarding the precise significance, and the regulations
for the use of the symbol, at any particular time should therefore
be sought from the IWS.

At the time of writing (June 1967) the introduction of a new
joint promotion scheme, designed to benefit every British company processing pure new wool, the British Pure New Wool Club,
has just been announced. Bona fide inquiries and applications
should be addressed to British Pure New Wool Club, c/o International Wool Secretariat, Wool House, Carlton Gardens,
London, S.W.1.

The Codemark

The purpose of this symbol, first publicized by the International Wool Secretariat in January 1968, is to identify yarns suitable for Woolmark products; manufacturers are thus assured that yarns accompanied by the mark comply with IWS Woolmark specifications.

Research

The IWS finances research all over the world in institutions such as research associations, and by individuals. In addition, IWS research scholars and fellows undertake investigations in the textile departments of universities.

In order to speed the application of research results, the IWS inaugurated a department known as Product Development and Technical Services. The staff of this department gives advice and training on production techniques and new processes, and seeks and encourages new uses for wool. In various parts of the world there are experimental plants where members of the staff of this department demonstrate easy-care processes to the local textile industry.

Of great importance to the British wool textile industry is the new IWS Technical Centre at Ilkley, which was opened in the latter part of 1968. Main objects of the Ilkley Centre are to improve the competitive end-use performance of a wide range of wool products, including apparel, carpets and blankets, and to develop new uses for wool. It must be stressed that these objects are not in competition with, but complementary to, the work of such organizations as the Commonwealth Scientific and Industrial Research Organization, and the Wool Industries Research Association.

The translation of laboratory research results into practical application for use in the factory demands a period of thorough development to ensure that no vestige of teething troubles—or as little as possible—remains when a new machine or method is introduced into the industry. During this period of development the man in the industry must be consulted, and the proximity of

Ilkley to the Yorkshire wool textile industry was one of the major factors in determining the site of the Technical Centre.

Education and Training

The Department of Education and Training concentrates its activities in the field of retail and technical training. Conferences are held for all sections of the retail trade concerned with wool products, and assistance is given to technical colleges and specialist teaching establishments running courses on such subjects as retail distribution. Encouragement is given to schools, particularly junior schools, in the promotion of hand knitting.

The Department publishes a variety of training aids, the particulars of which are given in a leaflet, *Facts about Pure New Wool*. Amongst these are (1967):

Books

A series of booklets describe in easily understood language modern developments in easy-care processes for wool: (a) *Easy Washability*, (b) *Durable Pleating, Creasing and Flat Setting*, (c) *Mothproofing, Showerproofing and Stainproofing*.

The British Wool Cloth Sample Book contains actual samples of 14 types of woollen and worsted cloth, together with the weave plans and notes on the characteristics and uses of the cloths.

The Scottish Wool Cloth Sample Book contains similar samples of and information on twenty-two characteristic woollen and worsted cloths produced by the Scottish industry, and a useful survey of the industry.

Wall Charts

The British Wool Cloth Display Card illustrates by means of samples the successive stages of woollen and worsted manufacture.

Wool and Knitting illustrate the production of hand knitting wools, and gives advice on knitting and on washing the fabric.

Facts About Hand Knitting Wool is published by the Department of Education and Training on behalf of the Hand Knitting Wool Council. A useful free leaflet.

Filmstrips

Wool Cloth Manufacture (black and white) shows stages in the manufacture of woollen and worsted cloth.

Wool Carpets for Modern Homes (colour) shows designs of wool carpets in room settings, and includes descriptions of Axminsters and Wiltons, and advice on selection, care, and stain removal.

The Paris Couture Collections in Wool—Spring/Summer 1967 (colour) illustrates in 84 colour photographs a representative selection of the pure new wool clothes shown in Paris.

Films

16 mm sound films are available free on loan to the retail trade, the industry, and appropriate technical colleges.

The Wonder of Wool (colour) describes the structure and properties of the wool fibre, manufacturing processes, characteristics of wool textiles, and easy-care finishes.

Woolmark (colour) explains the symbol, its significance to retailer and consumer, and the quality control of Woolmark merchandise.

Wool Makes its Mark (colour) illustrates the development of the Woolmark operation.

International Wool Menswear Office

This Department of the IWS World Headquarters has two principal objectives:

(1) *Information.* To provide information for the Press and for the trade about developments in wool menswear and to review and forecast trends in yarn, cloth, and clothes.

(2) *Marketing.* Through local branch directors, to assist spinners, weavers, clothing manufacturers, tailors, and retailers to

make profitable use of the latest styling and technical developments in wool.

Other IWS Activities

The reader is referred to the index of this book for some other activities of the IWS—such as joint campaigns with industry, design groups, etc. Articles in the *Wool Science Review* series are listed amongst the literature at the end of each appropriate processing section.

THE PRESS

The wool textile industry is well served by the Press, both trade journals and newspapers. The active and healthy co-operation between the Wool Textile Industry Central Press Office is mentioned on p. 62; apart from this there is a ready and spontaneous interchange of views, and a good understanding, between journalists and members of the industry.

Anybody wishing to keep himself abreast of general and technical events in the industry should scan through the issues of the *Wool Record*, a lively weekly journal which, as well as reporting hard news, does not hesitate to criticize the activities of the Government, other industries, and other countries. The *Wool Record* also produces occasional separately bound surveys of particular subjects, such as the Scottish industry, dyeing and finishing, man-made fibres in the wool textile industry, and publishes an *Annual Trade Review*.

Local papers in textile districts all over the country are, of course, sources of textile information and news for their own districts. But as so much of the industry is concentrated in Yorkshire, particularly the Bradford district, the daily papers to which the inquirer should turn for news of the wool textile industry in general are the *Yorkshire Post* and the *Telegraph and Argus*. In addition to their daily news and reports both of these papers publish an *Annual Trade Review*.

The names and addresses of some textile journals are listed below.

The Ambassador, monthly; 49 Park Lane, London, W.1. Textile and fashion news.

Carpet Review, monthly; 222 Strand, London, W.C.2. Incorporating *Floorcovering Review*.

Hosiery Times, monthly; Mercury House, Acton Square, Salford, 5, Lancs. The journal of the Hosiery and Knitwear Industry.

Hosiery Trade Journal, monthly; Head Office: 11 Millstone Lane, Leicester; Northern Office: 274/278 The Corn Exchange, Fennel Street, Manchester, 4.

International Dyer, fortnightly; published by Textile Press Ltd., Old Colony House, South King Street, Manchester, 2.

Texstyle, bi-monthly; 91 Kirkgate, Bradford, 1. Cloth styles and designs.

Textile Manufacturer, monthly; Emmott & Co. Ltd., 31 King Street West, Manchester, 3. Sub-titled "Materials, Processes, Production, Management".

Textile Mercury, fortnightly; Mercury House, Acton Square, Salford, 5, Lancs.

Textile Month, monthly; Textile Press (1955) Ltd., Old Colony House, South King Street, Manchester, 2. Embraces all fibres and processes. First issued in January 1968, it replaced three existing journals: Man-made Textiles, Skinner's Record of the Man-made Fibres Industry, and Textile Recorder.

Textile Weekly, Textile Press Ltd., Old Colony House, South King Street, Manchester, 2.

Wool Record and Textile World, weekly; 91 Kirkgate, Bradford, 1. Published by Textile Press, Ltd.

Wool Textile Industry, monthly; 222 Strand, London, W.C.2. News, technical and general articles, fashion.

NATIONAL SHEEP BREEDERS' ASSOCIATION

This Association, which was formed in 1892, represents breeders of sheep at the national level, and is a non-profit making organization. The Executive Council comprises representatives of the breed societies and individual members, and there are several sub-committees, each concerned with a particular aspect of the Association's work. In 1965–6 there were thirty-two affiliated sheep breed societies, three associated societies, and about 600 individual members.

An important aspect of the Association's work is to keep the Ministry of Agriculture, Fisheries, and Food, and the Scottish Office, aware of the difficulties that have to be met by sheep farmers, and of the effects that government policies may have on this important industry. The export of British sheep, particularly breeding stock, can be a valuable asset to the country provided that financial and other difficulties are not prohibitive. Thus the Ministry can help by negotiating to ease the restrictions imposed by countries that should benefit by importing British sheep. The Association seeks to improve this situation by arranging for British sheep to be exhibited at shows throughout the world.

The Association also advises the Ministry and the Scottish Office regarding the import of foreign breeds, and the controls that should be applied to such imports in the interests of British sheep farmers.

A *Year Book* was published in 1961–2, and since then news of particular interest has been sent to members from time to time. A *News Letter* containing articles by experts in their own field is sent to members and to educational establishments three or four times a year.

In co-operation with the principal agricultural show societies the handbook *British Pure Bred Sheep* was published in 1946; it has been brought up to date and superseded by *British Sheep* (see p. 192). The Association also maintains a *Bibliography of Sheep*, the information in which is freely available to bona fide inquirers.

A report entitled *Sheep Recording and Progeny Testing* has been produced in co-operation with the National Farmers' Union for England and Wales, and the Scottish NFU, the British Wool Marketing Board, the Sheep Development Association, the National Agricultural Advisory Service, and the Livestock Records Bureau.

The Sheep Breeders' associations and societies associated or affiliated at August 1966, are shown in the following list:

Blackface Sheep Breeders' Association.
Black Welsh Mountain Sheep Breeders' Association.
Bluefaced Leicester Sheep Breeders' Association.
Border Leicester Sheep Breeders, Society of.
Cheviot Sheep Society.
Clun Forest Sheep Breeders' Society Ltd.
Dales-Bred Sheep Breeders' Association Ltd.
Dartmoor Sheep Breeders' and Flock Book Association.
Devon Closewool Sheep Breeders' Society.
Dorset Down Sheep Breeders' Association.
Dorset Horn Sheep Breeders' Association.
Exmoor Horn Sheep Breeders' Society.
Hampshire Down Sheep Breeders' Association.
Herdwick Sheep Breeders' Association.
Hill Radnor Flock Book Society.
Kent and Romney Marsh Sheep Breeders' Association.
Kerry Hill Flock Book Society.
Leicester Longwool Sheep Breeders' Association.
Lincoln Longwool Sheep Breeders' Association.
Llanwenog Sheep Society.
Lonk Sheep Breeders' Association.
North Country Cheviot Sheep Society.
Oxford Down Sheep Breeders' Association.
Romney Marsh (*see above under* Kent and Romney Marsh)
Rough Fell Sheep Breeders' Association.
Ryeland Flock Book Society Ltd.

Shropshire Sheep Breeders' Association and Flock Book
   Society.

South Devon Flock Book Society.

Southdown Sheep Society.

Suffolk Sheep Society.

Swaledale Sheepbreeders' Association.

Teeswater Sheepbreeders' Association.

Welsh Half-Bred Sheepbreeders' Association.

Welsh Mountain Flock Book Society.

Wensleydale Longwool Sheepbreeders' Association.

White Face Dartmoor Sheep Breeders' Association.

The addresses of the above associations and societies can be
supplied by the National Sheep Breeders Association, or be ascertained from the handbook, *British Sheep*, which should be
available through any public library.

In addition, there are about ten smaller breed organizations
which, for one reason or another, cannot be affiliated or associated.

BRITISH WOOL MARKETING BOARD

The British Wool Marketing Board, which was set up in 1950,
consists of twelve members representing the wool growers, and
three members appointed by the Government. The Board or-
ganizes the marketing of the British clip, and provides a means of
liaison between the wool growers and the wool textile industry.
The wool auction sales, which are held at Bradford, London,
Leicester, Exeter, Edinburgh, and Belfast at various times throughout the year, are conducted by the Committee of London Wool
Brokers on behalf of the British Wool Marketing Board.

The Board's main objectives are:

(1) To stabilize returns to growers through standard prices and
    a stabilization fund.

(2) To achieve maximum prices for British wool by presenting
    it in ways which meet users' needs—e.g. national grades,
    offerings spread throughout the year by quantity and type.

(3) To reduce or minimize costs within the marketing channel.
(4) To improve the physical condition of the British wool clip by price incentives and grower education.
(5) To promote consumer demand for articles made from British wool.

For further information the reader is referred to the Board's brochure, *The British Wool Marketing Board: its organization and operations.*

CHAPTER 4

Research For The Wool Textile Industry

SCIENTIFIC RESEARCH LEVY

In November 1946 the Wool Working Party suggested that research for the wool textile industry required closer co-ordination and should be supported by a Statutory Levy. An Order (Statutory Instrument No. 1739) made under the Industrial Organization and Development Act, 1947, imposed a Scientific Research Levy on firms carrying on productive processes in the wool textile industry, and on persons dealing in the raw materials of that industry. A voluntary Council, the Wool Textile Research Council, was set up in 1950 to implement the suggestion of the Wool Working Party. The levy is collected by the Board of Trade and originally was passed on to the Wool Textile Research Council for meeting the expenses of work sponsored by the Council. In 1968, however, it was decided that this Council should be embodied in and its functions taken over by the new Wool Industries Research Association Council.

The greater part of the proceeds of the levy (the Wool Textile Industry (Scientific Research) Levy) is generally received by the Wool Industries Research Association, the remainder being allocated to such establishments as the universities of Bradford, Leeds, and Manchester (the Departments of Textile Industries, Textile Chemistry, etc.), Huddersfield, and other colleges of technology, and the Scottish Woollen Technical College, Galashiels. Grants may in fact be made to any organization undertaking research in the general interests of the wool textile industry. Contributions are also made to the Textile Institute's Publication Fund, the

Society of Dyers and Colourists, to trade effluent research at the Water Pollution Research Laboratory, Stevenage, and to the Wool Textile Industry Central Press Office.

When the Wool Textile Delegation, which represents about 85 per cent of the industry, considers that an increase of funds available for research is required, this body consults with other bodies representing persons in the industry liable to the levy, and puts the matter to the Board of Trade. An Amendment to the Wool Textile Industry (Scientific Research Levy) Order is then laid before Parliament.

WOOL INDUSTRIES RESEARCH ASSOCIATION
Torridon, Headingley Lane, Leeds, 6

This industrial research association was the first to be set up on the initiative of its own industry. It was incorporated in September 1918 under the aegis of the Department of Scientific and Industrial Research (which became the Ministry of Technology in April 1965) as the British Association for the Woollen and Worsted Industries, and changed its name to Wool Industries Research Association in June 1930.

Membership of the Association is voluntary, but any firm paying the statutory levy for research (see p. 111) is entitled to ordinary membership free of charge; so virtually all firms in the wool textile industry having processing machinery, or which handle a substantial amount of raw wool, are ordinary members. There are other forms of membership the terms and regulations concerning which are reviewed as the occasion arises.

The Wool Industries Research Association Council, the new single body which was set up in 1968 to replace both the Wool Textile Research Council (see p. 111) and the old Wool Industries Research Association Council, is composed mainly of men nominated by the official organizations of the industry. The day-to-day running of the Association is through a board of management responsible only to the Council; as chief executive of the Association, the Director of Research is a member of this board.

The Industrial Processes Research Group at Wira (see note below) includes the processing departments which correspond largely with the sections of the industry. The General Sciences Research Group includes all the scientific disciplines on which the fundamental research programme is based. The Member Service Groups provide consulting and advisory services, and promote Wira and other developments in the industry; included in these groups are the Library and Publication and Training facilities. The names of some of the departments give an indication of the wide scope of the work done in the laboratories: Scouring and Combing; Woollen Carding and Spinning; Worsted Drawing and Spinning; Weaving; Dyeing and Finishing; a Consulting and Advisory Service for members; Project Assessment; Testing; Mathematics and Statistics; Electronics; and Engineering. The research programme is given definite commercial objectives; a research committee, which includes business executives, filters the many ideas coming from industry, academic institutions, and Wira itself.

The Association has introduced many new and modified methods of processing and testing; new machines and instruments are developed, and may be patented, some of them being put into commercial production. Examples of new weaving machinery are given on p. 150, and of testing devices on p. 171. The development of testing methods and devices has always been regarded as a valuable facet of Wira's work. Some of these innovations provide a rapid method of testing that can be used during the course of processing, and thus be incorporated in a quality control scheme. Some of the chemical tests now available for general use are listed on p. 172.

Industrial research becomes effective only after it has been satisfactorily communicated to and has been adopted for use by the industry. The communication of research results to the industry is thus of paramount importance. Informal lecture–discussion meetings, for all levels in the mill from directors to foremen and overlookers, and other types of meeting and conference, are held in the lecture hall of the administration block which was completed in 1966.

The main link between Wira and its members is a group of industrial advisers whose main objective is to promote Wira and other developments within the industry. They also provide technical advice to members on day-to-day problems. The industrial advisers' contact with members is at the highest level and, together with the Wira directorate, provide a feed-back of information on the commercial objectives required of the research programme. Research staff have frequent contact with industry but are mainly concerned with the progress of the research projects in hand.

Members are kept informed about research results by means of a series of publications based on the *Wira News*, which aim to provide maximum impact whilst ensuring feed-back of industry's interests and needs. A useful service for members is *Wira's Current Awareness Notes*—known as *Wira Scan*. These notes are produced by the library staff who scan the major textile periodicals published both in this country and abroad, noting items of particular interest to the wool textile industry. Only brief particulars are given of each item, so that the notes made from a fortnight's periodicals can be read in a few minutes. Further information on any item can be obtained by contacting the library, or photostats of complete articles can be supplied for retention (in order to comply with copyright regulations these are charged for).

A comprehensive library covering the scientific and technical aspects of wool textile and allied subjects, both books and journals (foreign as well as British), is maintained for the benefit of the staff and of members. Abstracts of articles applying to the production and processing of wool and other animal fibres in British and foreign journals are prepared for the Textile Institute; these appear in *Textile Abstracts*, the publication which in March 1967 replaced the abstracts section of the *Journal*, and, of course, are available to members of Wira.

In order to provide a close link with the Scottish industry the Wira Scottish Branch Laboratory was established at Galashiels in 1945. Housed on the top floor of the Production Unit of the Scottish Woollen Technical College, it comprised three departments—Technical, Physics, and Chemistry, each of which also undertook consulting and research work. The textile machinery of the Technical College has been at the disposal of the Branch Laboratory for experimental work. In 1968 the research activities of this laboratory were transferred to the central Wira laboratories at Leeds and the Scottish Branch Laboratory was renamed Member Service Unit—Scotland. A team of industrial advisers based on Galashiels provides a first-class member service facility and includes arrangements for consulting, advisory, and test services at Galashiels. Promotion of new developments and contact at top level remain the industrial advisers' chief objectives.

The staff of Wira numbers about 200, some 60 of these being graduates or similarly qualified; there is thus a wide choice of interesting and worth-while careers open to prospective members of the staff. Vacancies occur for chemists and physicists, who may be employed on both fundamental and applied research, and for textile technologists to work in the processing departments on research and development projects, and also on fibre microscopy and textile testing. There are also occasional vacancies for mathematicians, statisticians, biologists, electronic engineers, mechanical engineers, and in the engineering drawing office and workshop. Improvements in member services and communications are providing vacancies for industrial advisors and publicity personnel.

Publications

Certain books published by Wira are available to the general public and can be bought through book shops; these have been included in the appropriate lists at the end of the processing sections earlier in this book. Others are confidential to members, sometimes only for a limited period.

Wira maintains a long-established and fruitful liaison with both the technical and lay Press, and distributes Press Releases annually and when topical news is available. Bona fide inquirers should apply for such literature as the yearly report of the Director of Research, and other open literature including a brief description of the Association.

Note

Those who have occasion to write about the Association should note that the term W.I.R.A. (with full points) was for a long time used as the recognized abbreviation of Wool Industries Research Association; the term WIRA (without full points) was registered as the Trade Mark of the Association and has been used as a prefix for patented devices, e.g. WIRA Fibre Diagram Machine (see p. 171). Since early 1968, however, the practice has been for all references to the Association to be by use of the term Wira.

OTHER TEXTILE RESEARCH ASSOCIATIONS

Space requirements unfortunately preclude any description of the other textile research associations, but their names and addresses are:

> Cotton, Silk, and Man-Made Fibres Research Association, Shirley Institute, Didsbury, Manchester, 20.
> Hosiery and Allied Trades Research Association, Thorneywood, Gregory Boulevard, Nottingham.
> Lace Research Association, Glaisdale Drive West, Bilborough, Nottinghamshire.
> British Launderers' Research Association, Hill View Gardens, Hendon, London, N.W.4.

Note

The British Hat and Allied Feltmakers Research Association, Stanley House, Manchester Road, Audenshaw, Manchester, closed down in 1967.

INFORMATION ON CAREERS IN THE RESEARCH ASSOCIATIONS

A booklet giving information on opportunities for careers in the research associations, educational qualifications required, training facilities, and starting salaries, entitled *Careers in the Industrial Research Associations*, has been produced by the Committee of Directors of Research Associations, 24 Buckingham Gate, London, S.W.1. Inquiries should be sent to the Secretary of the Committee.

Another booklet on the research associations, *Combining for Research*, is published by the Ministry of Technology.

RESEARCH BY MANUFACTURERS OF TEXTILE MACHINERY

Much research and development is done by the manufacturers of textile machinery. Such organizations, in addition to originating their own inventions, can play an important part in furthering the progress of inventions brought to them for development. Such a device may have been translated into a practicable machine that will perform the required operation efficiently; but the firm which will manufacture and market it is in a position to make modifications and final developments to ensure that it will be commercially practicable. The design of the machine put on to the market must, in addition to many other considerations, take into account its servicing and the supply of spare parts after it has been installed in the processing factory.

The principle of autolevelling in worsted drawing (see p. 138) offers an example of a revolutionary invention being progressed from the original conception to eventual production on a commercial basis. The inventor, Mr. (now Dr.) G. F. Raper, brought his idea to the laboratories of the Wool Industries Research Association for the early stages of development; the machine was then subjected to proving trials in one of the factories of Messrs. Patons and Baldwins Ltd.; finally, Messrs. Prince-Smith & Stells Ltd. (a member of the Stone–Platt Group of textile machinery manufacturers) produced a marketable machine in 1953 which was eminently satisfactory for the wool textile industry and remarkably free from the teething troubles sometimes suffered by a completely new type of machine. Modern types of autolevelling unit are now incorporated in Prince-Smith & Stells' range of drawing machinery known as the Speed-O-Gill series, and in their Uniflex System of drawing and spinning.

A more recent example of research and development conducted by the Stone–Platt Group is the completion of a new system for the manufacture of semi-worsted yarn, a method of worsted yarn manufacture in which the process of combing is eliminated. The new system was demonstrated in 1967 at TMM (Research) Ltd., Helmshore, the central research unit of the Stone–Platt Group. With this system the number of operations is reduced to four or five compared with about twelve in a conventional system. Economies thus result from the reduced number of operatives required and from the adaptability of the system.

An example of the conventional method of cap spinning (see p. 139) being advanced to a high degree of efficiency by machinery manufacturers is given by Prince-Smith & Stells' new (1967) high-speed cap spinner, KCS2. An outstanding feature of this machine is the specially designed spindle unit in which vibration is virtually eliminated by means of divorcing the rotating package from the stationary spindle; the grease-packed ball-bearing unit enables spindle speeds of up to 12,000 r.p.m. to be achieved.

UNIVERSITY OF LEEDS

A small flock of Tasmanian Merino sheep is maintained at the University experimental farm, and their fleeces demonstrate that the best quality of fine wool can be grown in this country if sheep of the right genetic kind are chosen. The crossing of this Merino stock with Cheviots has also resulted in some very fine quality wool. The work has been in the charge of Mr. H. B. Carter of the Agricultural Research Council and an honorary Research Fellow in the Department of Textile Industries.

In fibre science a great deal of attention is being paid to the structure and reactivity of wool and man-made fibres, chromatography being a valuable technique in this type of work. Other sophisticated tools being used in the Department for the study of textile fibres are the electron microscope, the scanning electron microscope, X-ray techniques, amino-acid analysis, electrophoresis, ultracentrifugation, and electron spin resonance.

In textile engineering, work is directed towards the development of new machines and processing techniques, and the better understanding of the properties of textile yarns and fabrics. This includes work on the degreasing of wool, carding, drawing and spinning, weaving, finishing, the production of wool/shoddy cloths, and other processing techniques, including knitting and non-woven fabrics.

Research is also carried out on all aspects of fibre processing including raw materials, yarn manufacture, weaving, knitting, the production of fibre-woven and non-woven textiles, finishing, and quality control. There is an active group dealing with problems of automatic control of processing, machine noise, and the geometry and properties of all forms of textiles.

Research is conducted on behalf of the Federation of British Carpet Manufacturers, and also on behalf of the Clothing Institute. In clothing research the aims are (i) to foster the entry of an increasing number of suitable graduates into the clothing industry, (ii) to investigate and advise on day-to-day technical problems, (iii) to provide basic data for the solution of longer-term problems, and for increasing the productivity and technical efficiency of the clothing industry as a whole.

Research in the Department of Colour Chemistry and Dyeing is concerned with a wide variety of subjects including fibre-reactive dye and surface chemistry, photochemistry, diffusion studies, reaction kinetics, nucleation studies, and organic synthesis. Amongst the specialized equipment in the Department are ultraviolet, infrared and visible recording spectrophotometers, reflectance colorimeters, particle size analysis equipment of various kinds, equipment for polarography, and radio-isotope scintillation counting equipment. There is also a wide range of semi-full-scale production equipment for the application of dyes, enabling research to be done on technological as well as fundamental scientific problems.

UNIVERSITY OF BRADFORD

In the Department of Textile Industries a study is being made of the potentialities of various types of British wools for the production of worsted fabrics used (i) alone, (ii) in combination with other wool types, (iii) in combination with man-made fibres. Amongst other current (1967) investigations in processing techniques are a theoretical and experimental study of woolcombing with special reference to fibre breakage, the use of a simple mechanical device in blending, several investigations in worsted drawing and spinning, and research and development work in fabric design and colour using all fibres and methods of manufacture.

The structure of keratin (the wool substance) and related natural and synthetic fibrous materials is being studied by physical and chemical methods:

(a) Infrared, spectroscopic, and X-ray diffraction techniques, as well as electron microscopy, are being used in a fundamental research programme to study the structure of the morphological components of wool and related substances.

(b) Keratins are being degraded into simpler components by chemical means; and to serve as models for keratin a programme based on the synthesis of polypeptides and cross-linked polyamides has been initiated. These materials are examined by the techniques applicable to classical protein chemistry, e.g. ion-exchange chromatography, paper chromatography, and electrophoresis.

NATIONAL RESEARCH DEVELOPMENT CORPORATION
Kingsgate House, 66–74, Victoria Street, London, S.W.1

The Corporation, whose members are appointed by the Ministry of Technology and hold important positions in science, industry, and commerce, is an independent public Corporation, not a government department. It is financed by means of government loans, and, being required to balance its accounts in the long term, it has to conduct its activities on a sound commercial basis.

The purpose of the NRDC is to promote the adoption by industry of new products and processes invented in government laboratories, universities, and elsewhere, advancing money where necessary to bring them to a commercially viable stage. It speeds up technological advance by investing money with industrial firms for the development of their own inventions and projects.

Public inventions are the proper concern of the Corporation; but private inventions, the development of which, in the opinion of the Corporation, would be in the public interest, are statutorily qualified for support.

NRDC does not itself manufacture or trade, nor does it have its own research or development facilities. It arranges for the development of inventions by placing contracts with industry, with universities or private research laboratories, or by setting up a development company for such purpose. "Exploitation" of its inventions is normally arranged for by the grant of licences to manufacturers under the relevant patent rights.

The Corporation co-operates with the wool textile industry in many ways, one example being (in conjunction with the Wool Industries Research Association) the problem of effluent disposal.

Publications

The Corporation has a large portfolio of inventions, and welcomes inquiries from industry about them. It publishes, every 6 months, a bulletin—*Inventions for Industry*.

Copies of the annual *Statutory Report* can be obtained from HMSO.

COMMONWEALTH SCIENTIFIC AND INDUSTRIAL RESEARCH ORGANIZATION

The CSIRO undertakes research relating to primary and secondary industry in Australia. Its work, in laboratories and field stations in all states, is concerned with the problems of various industries and with the basic sciences on which these industries depend. There are three divisions of CSIRO comprising the Wool

Research Laboratories. Their work covers fundamental research on the wool fibre, and all operations, including the branding of wool while on the sheep, its handling, transportation, processing, testing, and final use in the form of consumer goods. Good co-operation is maintained between these laboratories, and such institutions as the International Wool Secretariat and the Wool Industries Research Association, so the research findings are inevitably important to the British wool textile industry.

The three divisions are:

Division of Protein Chemistry

343 Royal Parade, Parkville, N.2., Victoria

This division undertakes research on the structure and chemistry of wool and on wool processes which do not require the use of conventional textile processing equipment, or which exploit the special knowledge that has been built up in the Division.

Division of Textile Physics

The Hermitage, 338 Blaxland Road, Ryde, NSW

This division gives special attention to the physical properties of wool. The research embraces studies of the mechanical and water sorption properties of wool fibres, associated practical applications to processes and the development of improved testing methods.

Division of Textile Industry

Princes Highway, Belmont, Geelong, Victoria

This division is concerned mainly with textile processes designed to confer new properties on wool and with related studies.

WOOL RESEARCH IN NEW ZEALAND

At Lincoln, near Christchurch, a new laboratory building was opened in 1967 to house two separate research institutions: the

Wool Research Organisation of New Zealand (Inc.) and the New Zealand Wool Industries Research Institute. The postal address of both institutions is: Private Mail Bag, Christchurch, New Zealand.

Wool Research Organisation of New Zealand (Inc.)

The Organisation, which was established as a research association under the Incorporated Societies' Act on 19 January 1961, is an autonomous body supported by equal annual grants from the New Zealand Wool Board and the New Zealand Government. Its projects are accordingly selected with a view to benefiting wool growers and the New Zealand economy.

The field of research includes fibre structure and properties, fibre modification (by chemical means), fibre products (most important—optimum methods of constructing carpets from New Zealand wools), and material handling. Examples of handling processes are shearing, classing, pressing, transport to store, showing for auction, and dumping (pressing bales to higher densities and binding with steel wires or bands) to conserve space on board ship. In the slipe wool industry, one handling problem is the pulling of wool from sheep skins. Improved methods of doing this are investigated in collaboration with the New Zealand Leather and Shoe Research Association.

New Zealand Wool Industries Research Institute (Inc.)

Co-operative research for the wool manufacturing industry began in 1937 with the formation of the New Zealand Wool Manufacturers' Research Association. Its objects were to assist the wool textile mills with their manufacturing problems and to conduct applied research. The Association, which was financed jointly by member firms and the Government, was first housed in the University of Otago, Dunedin. In 1945 it was separately incorporated as the New Zealand Woollen Mills Research Association (Inc.), and in 1947 the New Zealand Wool Board began to make a yearly grant. In 1957 membership was extended to include commission woolscourers, and so the title was changed to the present more appropriate New Zealand Wool Industries Research Institute (Inc.).

The Institute's research programme includes wool in relation to manufacturing (particularly crossbred wool), carding, combing and spinning, woolscouring (including the recovery of lanolin and effluent treatment), testing, and investigation of members' problems.

INTERNATIONAL WOOL SECRETARIAT

Research conducted by the IWS is referred to on p. 102.

CHAPTER 5

Wool Processing

SHEARING, CLASSING, AND SORTING

Machine shearing is now the normal method, but blade shearing (hand) is still used for small batches and for stud animals which may require particular attention. The first operation in shearing is to cut away those parts of the fleece that would degrade the standard of the whole. These are known by such terms as locks, crutchings, clags, daggings, and bellies, and together with other similar pieces are put aside to be marketed separately. The method of shearing so that the whole fleece comes away is described in Bowen's book and others listed at the end of this section. There will still be attached to the fleece some parts that would detract from the value of the whole, and these are trimmed away— an operation known as skirting. The amount of wool removed in skirting depends on the individual fleece in relation to the standard being aimed at. Thus a relatively good fleece might be skirted fairly drastically to keep it in a high class, and a poorer fleece might be skirted more lightly and consigned to a lower class.

Classing is a preliminary grading of complete fleeces as opposed to sorting in which the fleece is pulled apart and separated into different sorts. Classing is normally done directly after shearing in the country of origin; sorting is normally done in the country or district of manufacture. Wool differs not only between one flock and another, and one animal and another, but also between different parts of the whole fleece. Thus in classing a fleece, the regularity of the following attributes have to be taken into account: quality (fineness), fibre length, soundness (tensile strength), colour (degree of "whiteness"), yield (estimated proportion of usable wool and waste in the form of grease, sweat, vegetable and mineral matter), and an attribute known as "style", which largely comprises handle, lustre, and crimp (waviness of the fibres and staples). The categories of classification are determined partly by the requirements of the section of the processing industry for which the wool may be destined. Thus there is a broad division between wool for worsted, which has to be long enough for combing; and that for woollen, which can be extremely short.

In sorting, the fleece is separated into various "sorts", "matchings", or "qualities" according to the physical attributes mentioned above. A sorter should therefore have a good knowledge of the physical features of wool fibres.

In addition to being shorn from live sheep, wool is "pulled" from dead ones. When taken from the skin of animals that have been slaughtered for mutton the wool is known as "slipes" or skin wool; wool from animals that have died from natural causes is known as "dead wool".

Some Literature on Shearing, Classing, Sorting, and Wool Marketing

BOWEN, G., *Wool Away: the technique and art of shearing*, Whitcombe & Tombs (New Zealand), 3rd edn., 1964. Bowen, a leading exponent of the art of shearing, describes many breeds of sheep, how to shear them, and the properties of the various fleeces.

COWLEY, C. E., *Classing the Clip*, Angus & Robertson, Sydney, 4th edn., 1944. A handbook by a former Lecturer-in-Charge, Sheep and Wool Department, Sydney Technical College.

HAIGH, H. *The Work of the Woolman*, E. & F. N. Spon, 1952. Written largely for the benefit of the apprentice starting in the industry. Work in the warehouse, and wool sorting. British wools and their uses in manufacture.

HENDERSON, A. E., *Wool and Woolclassing*, A. H. & A. W. Reed (New Zealand), 1965. Distributed in Britain by Bailey Bros. & Swinfen Ltd., 48 Upper Thames Street, London, E.C.4.

PONTING, K. G., *Wool Marketing*, Pergamon Press, 1966. This book is useful for the textile departments of universities and technical colleges, for agricultural colleges, and all interested in the marketing of wool. Marketing methods in different parts of the world are discussed; valuable conclusions and suggestions for the future are drawn.

RAINNIE, G. F. (Ed.), *The Woollen and Worsted Industry: an economic analysis*, Oxford University Press, 1965. Chapter 1 (by Rainnie, G. F.) is on "Raw materials and markets". Appendix A (by Brothwell, J. F.) is on "The London wool futures market".

THE WOOL FIBRE

The wool fibre was not studied thoroughly and systematically by the scientist before 1920, so some of the more obscure and interesting properties of wool, such as the heat of wetting and the mechanism of felting, are discussed authoritatively only in books and articles written since, say, the mid-1920's.

Both the length and diameter of a wool fibre are of great importance in processing, and the large variety of yarns and fabrics produced by the industry results partly from the wide range of these dimensions. Fibre length varies from the inch or so of fine Merino to 12 or 14 in. of the Lincoln. Diameter* ranges from about $0 \cdot 0005$ in. in fine Merino to about $0 \cdot 0025$ in. in Lincoln. Wool fibres are crimped or wavy in three dimensions, and the cross-section is slightly oval, the ovality rotating in conformation with the crimp.

The fibre consists basically of a cortex, composed of pointed cells set in an amorphous material, covered by a system of overlapping scales. The number of scales varies from about 40,000 per in. in fine Merino to about 800 in Lincoln. Some fibres have a central medulla consisting largely of air.

The molecule of the wool substance, keratin, consists of atoms of carbon, hydrogen, oxygen, nitrogen, and sulphur arranged in

* Fibre diameter is usually measured in microns (μ): $1\ \mu = 1/1000$ mm.

long chains of simpler substances running the length of the fibre, these being joined together by short cross-chains. This chain formation is normally in a folded or crumpled state, but when the fibre is stretched, the whole structure gradually straightens out. Therein lies the secret of wool's elasticity and its power of recovery.

Although wool repels liquid water, it readily absorbs water vapour; in normal circumstances wool that feels perfectly dry may contain about 16 per cent of water, and can contain about 30 per cent without feeling wet. The phenomenon known as "heat of wetting" results in heat being produced when water vapour is absorbed (this serves a useful purpose when, wearing wool, you go from a warm dry atmosphere indoors to a cold damp atmosphere outside).

Broadly speaking the literature on wool fibres may be divided into the biology of wool growth and the physical and the chemical formation of the fibre. In addition to the following list of books, the early parts of the more general books, such as A. J. Hall's (p. 131), should be consulted.

Some Literature on the Wool Fibre

ALEXANDER, P., HUDSON, R. P., and EARLAND, C., *Wool, Its Chemistry and Physics*, Chapman & Hall, 2nd edn., 1964. For knowledgeable readers, particularly on such topics as adsorption of water by wool, the disulphite bond and formation of new cross-links. Useful bibliography.

APPLEYARD, H. M., *Guide to the Identification of Animal Fibres* (see p. 192).

ASTBURY, W. T., *Fundamentals of Fibre Structure*, Oxford University Press, 1933. Astbury had the art of making an abstruse subject such as this pleasurable and profitable for the uninitiated as well as the expert to read.

COOK, J. G., *Handbook of Textile Fibres*, Merrow Publishing Co., 3rd edn., 1964. A useful brief reference book covering the structure, properties and processing of textile fibres.

HEARLE, J. W. S., and PETERS, R. H., *Fibre Structure*, Butterworths, 1963. A textbook for fibre scientists.

MEREDITH, R., and WOODS, H. J., *Physical Properties of Textiles*, Part I, Textile Institute, 1957. An easily understood booklet.

MORTON, W. E., and HEARLE, J. W. S., *Physical Properties of Textile Fibres*, Butterworths, 1962. Suitable for the student.

ONIONS, W. J., *Wool: an introduction to its properties, varieties, uses, and production*, Benn, 1962. A standard work of authoritative information clearly written. The majority of the book is about the many aspects of the wool fibre and its production; 14 of the 278 pages are on the marketing of wool and 36 on wool processing.

PRESTON, J. M. (Ed.), *Fibre Science*, Textile Institute, 2nd edn., 1953. For the scientist and technologist. Chapters particularly on wool are: "Protein fibres" by F. O. Howitt and "Survey of the chemistry of keratin fibres" by J. B. Speakman.

STOVES, J. L., *Fibre Microscopy*, National Trade Press, 1957. The technique of microscopy applied to fibres.

URQUHART, A. R., and HOWITT, F. O. (Eds), *The Structure of Textile Fibres: an introductory study*, Textile Institute, 1953. The structure of textile fibres explained simply.

WILDMAN, A. B., *The Microscopy of Animal Textile Fibres* (see p. 192).

WOODS, H. J., *Physics of Fibres: an introductory survey*, Institute of Physics, 1955. For the textile scientist. Mainly on the natural fibres.

International Wool Secretariat Articles

The following articles in the International Wool Secretariat's series, *Wool Science Review*, are intended mainly for the scientist and technologist:

WARBURTON, F. L., Physical properties of wool fibres: wool–water relations, No. 16, p. 36, Nov. 1956.

KING, G., Physical properties of wool fibres: thermal properties of fibres and fabrics, No. 17, p. 33, July 1957.

LINCOLN, B., Physical properties of wool fibres: frictional properties, No. 18, p. 38, Oct. 1960.

FEUGHELMAN, M., and LUNNEY, H. W., Mechanical properties of the wool fibre and their relation to structure, Part 1, No. 20, p. 19, Dec. 1961; Part 2, No. 21, p. 14, Aug. 1962.

HOWITT, F. O., Wool Keratin; its chemical structure and reactions, Part 1, No. 21, p. 27, Aug. 1962; Part 2, No. 22, p. 3, March 1963; Part 3, No. 23, p. 23, July 1963; Part 4, No. 24, p. 16, Feb. 1964.

LUNNEY, H. W., and BAIRD, K., Mechanical properties of the wool fibre and their relation to structure, Part 3, No. 22, p. 15, March 1963.

FRASER, R. D. B. and MACRAE, T. P., The fine structure of wool keratin as revealed by X-ray diffraction, No. 25, p. 1, Sept. 1964.

DOBB, M. G., Electron microscopy of wool keratin, No. 28, p. 1, Nov. 1965.

JOHNSON, D. J., and SIKORSKI, J., The fine and ultra-fine structure of keratin, No. 29, p. 25, April 1966.

General Literature on Wool and its Processing

The following books are suitable for students and for those requiring general information on wool and its processing.

BERGEN, W. VON, *Wool Handbook* (see p. 192).

BREARLEY, A., *The Woollen Industry*, Pitman, 1965; and *Worsted*, Pitman, 1964. These two books, in the revived Common Commodities and Industries Series, are eminently suitable for students, teachers, and anyone interested in the subject. The processes in these sections of the industry are described, technical principles being introduced in such a way that all can understand.

COOK, J. G., *Sheer Magic: the story of textile fibres* (a Spotlight on Science Book, No. 4), Merrow Pub. Co., 1953. A booklet written by a scientist for the layman. One chapter is on fibre fundamentals, another specifically on wool.

HALL, A. J., *The Standard Handbook of Textiles*, Heywood, 6th edn., 1965. A standard book for students and general readers on textile fibres and their processing.

HALL, A. J., *A Student's Textbook of Textile Science*, Allman & Son, 1963. For students and prospective members of the textile industries.

KORNREICH, E., *Introduction to Fibres and Fabrics*, Heywood, 2nd edn., 1966. For the student; the emphasis is on fibre properties.

MARSH, J. T., *Textile Science: an introductory manual*, Chapman & Hall, 4th (revised) Impression, 1958. A standard work covering fibre properties and processing.

WELFORD, T., *Textile Student's Manual*, Pitman, 5th edn., 1966. For teacher and student.

The British Wool Manual, Harlequin Press, 2nd edn. The book has a wide scope including ancient sheep breeds, the wool fibre and its physical and chemical properties, and its processing.

British Wool Cloth Sample Book, International Wool Secretariat, 1966. This "book" consists of actual cloth samples together with weave diagrams and text giving some particulars of its manufacture. Of value to anyone wishing to know more about different types of cloth.

Scottish Wool Cloth Sample Book, International Wool Secretariat, 1966. Similar to the above but larger, and there is a brief introduction to the Scottish woollen industry.

Some Textile Dictionaries

Dictionary of Dyeing and Textile Printing, Newnes, 1961.

Dictionary of Textile Terms, German–English/English–German, Pergamon Press, 1956.

English–Russian Textile Dictionary, Fitzmatgiza, 1961.

"Mercury" Dictionary of Textile Terms, Textile Mercury, Salford.

Modern Textile Dictionary, Allen & Unwin, 1956.

Textile Terms and Definitions, Textile Institute, Manchester, 5th edn., 1963.

WORSTED YARN MANUFACTURE

The two main types of yarn manufacture in the wool textile industry are worsted and woollen. With the increased use of man-made fibres there is a danger of these terms being misused, so it is important to consider both the type of fibres in the yarn and the method of manufacture. At one time a worsted yarn was assumed to be all wool; a woollen yarn, on the other hand, has for long been made either from all wool or from a blend of wool and other fibres. Today, man-made fibres, either in a blend with wool fibres or by themselves, may be made into yarn on the worsted principle. The following remarks apply to the two principles of manufacture.

In the preparation and spinning of a worsted yarn one of the main objects is to lay the fibres as nearly as possible parallel in the final twisted formation; the yarn is thus smooth and there should be few protruding short fibres. The very short fibres are removed in combing, a process that is not used in woollen yarn manufacture. A typical worsted yarn is that used in a gabardine cloth; most hand knitting yarns, other than Shetland, are also worsted.

Woollen yarn preparation is designed to lay the fibres in a higgledy-piggledy formation, and the yarn is fuzzy due to the protrusion of fibre ends. Typical woollen yarns are those used for tweeds and blankets.

Wool Scouring

Raw wool may contain up to 50 per cent, or even more, of impurities such as wool grease or wax, suint (sweat), dung, urine, sand, vegetable matter, brands, and dips. The traditional method of cleansing the wool is by means of emulsion scouring, in which it passes through a series of tanks (known in the industry as bowls) containing solutions of soap and sodium carbonate (soda ash); the last bowl normally contains plain water for rinsing the wool. A synthetic detergent may be used instead of soap, and some alkali other than soda ash may be used.

The wool is passed through each bowl by mechanical rakes or forks which ideally should agitate the fibres as little as possible. Work at the Wool Industries Research Association (see p. 112) has stressed the importance of avoiding felting of the fibres at this stage and thus lessening fibre breakage in the subsequent carding process; Wira research has also shown that the main requirement at this stage is to wet the wool thoroughly—mechanical cleansing takes place more at the squeeze rollers between the bowls. After the last bowl the wool passes into a dryer where it is dried by hot air, again with as little agitation as possible.

An alternative method of scouring, first used in about 1955, was devised by the Commonwealth Scientific and Industrial Research Organization (see p. 121) with the object of reducing entanglement and felting; it is usually known as solvent scouring. In this method the wool is carried on a wire belt and is subjected to jets of solvent from above; it then passes between squeeze rollers and under water jets. The solvent removes the grease and some of the other impurities; most of the remainder is removed by the water jetting.

Wool Carbonizing

Wool that contains a lot of vegetable matter (burry wool) may be treated chemically after scouring. In this process (carbonizing) the wool is steeped in a dilute solution of sulphuric acid and then dried with hot air. This transforms vegetable matter to a brittle state in which it readily crumbles away after shaking and in subsequent processing.

Worsted Carding

The next process, carding, is designed to open up the wool after scouring and to remove vegetable matter. The fibres are teased apart with a progressively vigorous action by means of large rollers covered with steel teeth and pins. This also has a blending action, because the fibres are taken by some rollers and replaced, so that they are thoroughly distributed in the final web. This web is gathered into a sliver which passes into a cylindrical can.

The longer wools may be "prepared" instead of carded. Preparing comprises a series of gilling operations (see below).

Backwashing

There is a certain amount of dust and other impurities in the carded sliver, which has therefore to be cleansed in a backwashing machine, dried, and given a preliminary pin treatment by means of gilling. Oil is also added to facilitate subsequent processing. All of these treatments are combined in the backwashing machine.

Gilling

This is essentially a worsted process designed to lay the fibres parallel; it also enhances regularity because several slivers enter the machine together and emerge as one. The machine, a gill box ("box" is a common term for this type of machine) comprises essentially two pairs of rollers, the surface speed of the second pair being greater than that of the first pair, and between the two pairs of rollers a set of "fallers" carrying steel teeth which comb through the fibres (Fig. 6). The attenuation of the sliver resulting from the difference of roller speeds is known as drafting, a term used throughout drawing and spinning to denote "drawing out thinner".

There may be two stages of gilling between backwashing and combing. In addition, a machine known as a punch box, winds four slivers into one ball for mounting around the base of the Noble Comb.

Combing

The object of combing is to rid the carded sliver of very short fibres and of any remaining vegetable matter, and to align the other fibres in as parallel a formation as possible. The short fibres (noil) provide a valuable raw material for the woollen section of the industry. The proportion of top (the combed sliver) to noil is termed the tear in combing (pronounced "tare").

In the Noble Comb, the commonest combing machine in the United Kingdom, the carded slivers are fed in so that their

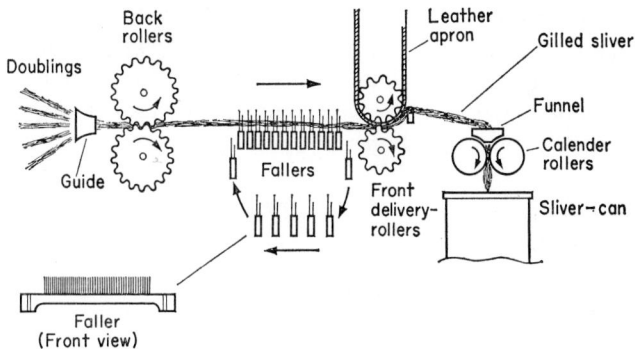

FIG. 6. Action of gill box in worsted open drawing. (From *Worsted* by Alan Brearley, Pitman.)

ends fall over two rotating horizontal steel rings ("circles") carrying steel pins set vertically, into which the sliver ends are "dabbed" by a brush. The smaller circle is inside and close to the large one, and rotates in the same direction. Thus as the two circles rotate, the pins holding the fibres separate. A combing action results, because a fringe of fibres, which has been combed through by the pins of the small circle, is left protruding from the large circle; and a similar fringe, combed by the pins of the large circle is left protruding from the small one. The action of the comb is duplicated, there being two small circles. Pairs of leathers and rollers remove the combed fringes and combine them into one composite combed sliver or top. The fibres in the pins of the small circles that are too short to be gripped by the withdrawing leathers are automatically removed and fed into cans; these are the noil. Similar short fibres in the large circle find their way to the inside of the large circle and pass into the small circle pins.

There are several other types of comb used to a lesser extent than the Noble, though no hard-and-fast rules can be given for their purposes. The Heilmann or French Comb is used for wools that are too short for the Noble, and is now used also for much longer wools. Normally these wools are drawn and spun by the French or Continental System: they are "dry spun", no oil being added, as is the practice with Noble combing. The machine does the same basic job as the Noble, combing the fibres and rejecting the very short ones, but it operates on what is known as the "nip" principle.

The Lister, which uses the "nip" principle in a different way, is used for long wools and also for alpaca and mohair. The Holden, or "square motion", comb is still used (1967) by one or two firms for very fine Merinos.

Some long wools, such as are used for linings, may be put through a series of gilling operations, as a preparation for the Lister or Noble Comb, instead of being carded.

After combing, whichever machine is used, the sliver is given one or two stages of gilling before being passed on to the drawing. These machines are known as finisher gill boxes.

In worsted processing the wool is usually not dyed until it has been combed. So if coloured top is required for drawing, it is dyed either as balls of top (top dyeing) or in hanks (slubbing dyeing). This inevitably disarranges to some extent the orderly arrangement of the fibres; so the dyed top is gilled again and generally recombed. Recombing is an operation in which some firms specialize.

Note

Literature referring to scouring, carding, gilling, and combing is listed after worsted drawing and spinning, and woollen yarn manufacture, because many books cover all these operations.

Worsted Drawing

The object of worsted drawing is to reduce the thick combed sliver to a thin "roving" suitable for spinning into a yarn. This is done by a series of operations involving "drafting" and "doubling"; drafting is the attenuation of the sliver mainly between two pairs of rollers; doubling is the combination of several slivers at the input of a machine to enhance regularity of thickness. There are now many methods of worsted drawing, which can be touched on only briefly in this book; they are simply yet authoritatively described in Brearley's book *Worsted* (see p. 130).

Before the Second World War there were four systems of drawing: (a) English (Bradford or Open), (b) Cone, (c) Continental (French or Porcupine), (d) Anglo-Continental (a combination of the traditional Bradford and Continental systems). This has virtually become obsolete. The systems now used are:

(a) *English or Open Drawing*

In this system there are up to eight stages of drafting and doubling in preparation for spinning. In the first two stages gill boxes are used, the machines incorporating two pairs of rollers for drafting, and fallers (see p. 134) for combing through the sliver between the pairs of rollers; the output sliver of the first gill box passes into a large can. That of the second gill box is wound on to a bobbin. Next come the draw boxes; these have drafting rollers and spindles, but there is no longer a combing action between them because there is now some twist in the slivers; the fibres between the rollers are controlled by means of small rollers resting on the sliver. Roving, the last stage of drawing, reduces the sliver to a size suitable for spinning.

(b) *Cone Drawing*

This is similar in general principle to open drawing, but less twist is used and a positive control of the bobbin on the spindle results in a softer roving suitable for the spinning of hosiery and similar yarns.

(c) *Continental Drawing*

Dry combed tops (without oil) are used for this method, and no twist is inserted at any stage; the fibres between the rollers are controlled by a "porcupine" roller fitted with steel pins or aprons, and a rubbing device. In the post-war New Continental System, autolevellers (see below) are used to reduce the number of stages of drawing. Continental drawing is used for hosiery and similar yarns.

(d) *Autolevelling*

During the Second World War the necessity for economizing in manpower prompted the Wool Industries Research Association (Wira) to investigate the possibilities of reducing the number of stages in open drawing, and a useful groundwork of research results was achieved. Pursuing this line of thought a man in the industry, Mr. (now Dr.) G. F. Raper, invented a most ingenious device for automatically controlling the regularity of thickness of the slivers during drawing; this enables the number of stages to be reduced from about eight to three or four. The device, the Raper Autoleveller, was developed through its early stages in co-operation with Wira, and after thorough proving trials and further development in a mill, was produced commercially by Prince-Smith & Stells Ltd., the Keighley textile machinery manufacturers. Since then, other similar devices have been devised and there are now many types of autoleveller.

The Raper Autoleveller used in drawing combined with the Ambler Superdraft method of spinning (see p. 139) became known as the New Bradford System of Drawing and Spinning.

Worsted Spinning

There are three main types of worsted spinning frame, each being suited to the production of a different type of yarn. These are the flyer, cap, and ring frame. The worsted mule is now little used.

The flyer frame operates on the same basic principle as the Saxony type of hand spinning wheel, which Arkwright mechanized in his water wheel. It incorporates a "flyer" rigidly attached to the spindle for inserting twist, and a bobbin on the spindle (not positively controlled) on which the yarn is wound. The flyer frame is used for spinning smooth yarns such as those for hand knitting, and for mohair and alpaca.

The cap spinning frame is so called because a steel cap, shaped like a long dome, controls the winding on of the yarn. The spindle is stationary and a brass tube rotates on it. Very high speeds are possible but the yarn is not so smooth as that spun by the flyer. The cap frame is used extensively for a wide range of yarns, chiefly medium and fine counts.

The ring spinning frame has a spindle rotating at the centre of a steel ring on which a small "traveller" rotates freely, carrying the yarn on its way to the bobbin. This frame runs at speeds intermediate between those of the flyer and the cap frames, and is used for several types of yarn; it is used as an alternative to the worsted mule for wool drawn on the Continental System.

The worsted spinning mule inserts the twist on the same basic principle as the woollen mule (see p. 142), but rollers are used for drafting the fibres. Once used fairly extensively for spinning French drawn rovings it has been largely superseded by the ring frame.

In about 1948 a revolutionary new method of spinning was introduced by Air Vice-Marshal Geoffrey Ambler, the device being known as the Ambler Superdraft. A small device, inserted behind the front pair of drafting rollers enables a very great increase in the ratio of the speeds of the two pairs of rollers. It is therefore possible to spin from a much thicker roving and so, amongst other advantages, two (as a rule) of the drawing stages can be eliminated. Other similar methods of high draft spinning have also been introduced.

WOOLLEN YARN MANUFACTURE

The differences between woollen and worsted yarn are given on p. 132; and wool scouring—used preparatory to woollen as well as worsted yarn manufacture—is also described briefly. In addition to virgin wool, other raw materials used for making woollen yarns are noils (short wool fibres rejected in worsted combing—see p. 135), waste from worsted and other yarn manufacture, shoddy, mungo, and various fibres other than wool, filament (continuous length) yarns being cut or broken into staple form.

Shoddy is obtained by pulling "soft" rags in a machine with spiked rollers; these rags are mainly knitted goods, and loosely woven cloths that have not been milled, or only lightly milled. Mungo is pulled from hard-woven and milled cloth, and felt.

Both shoddy and mungo may be pulled from unused manufacturing waste, tailor's clippings, old patterns, and similar material. Both can also be made from the collections of the rag and bone man or "tatter". Various stages of processing may therefore be necessary, such as sorting, carbonizing, shaking, dusting, washing, stripping and re-dyeing, and pulling.

Blending and Oiling

The first operation in woollen yarn manufacture (after any preliminary processes such as scouring, carbonizing, and rag pulling) is blending. The components are determined by the nature of the end product, which may be anything from a lightweight dress material to a heavy overcoating. The blend may contain cotton or man-made fibres, or may consist of nothing but undyed wool fibres, or wool fibres of various colours.

Machines with names such as willey, teazer, shaker, and fearnought are used for opening, cleansing, and teasing the material before blending. The traditional method of blending is to spread thin layers of the components on the floor, each layer being sprayed with oil from a can. The material is then taken from top to bottom and fed to a fearnought or similar machine. Modern systems (batch and continuous blending) make use of air ducts, rotary spreaders, devices for ensuring even distribution of oil, and other methods for blending and oiling, uniformly and efficiently.

Woollen Carding

Carding for woollen yarn is the same in some respects as that for worsted. The fibres are teased apart by spiked and pinned rollers on a large machine, and distributed evenly in a filmy web at the output end of the machine. In the "condenser" at the end of the card, this web is split into narrow strips, each of which is rubbed into a slubbing of the right size for spinning into a yarn. An important difference is that whereas carding is one of many stages in worsted yarn production, it is the heart of woollen yarn processing, being followed only by spinning. A woollen card is bigger too, consisting of two or three parts (scribbler, intermediate, and carder) as well as the final condenser. Different types of woollen yarn call for different types of carding machine for producing the slubbing. The differences are somewhat technical, but the main types of card are Yorkshire, Scottish, and Continental.

Several devices are available for crushing burrs and other impurities between precision-ground metal rollers under hydraulic pressure without harming the wool fibres; the crushed material drops out of the wool as it progresses through later stages of carding.

A device known as the Wira Autocount, developed in the laboratories of Wira, automatically exercises a control over the thickness of the slubbing being produced.

Woollen Spinning

There are two principal types of woollen spinning machine, the woollen mule and the woollen ring frame (which is steadily superseding the former).

The woollen mule is a direct descendant of Crompton's Mule of 1779 and Robert's Self-acting Mule of 1825, The carded slubbings, on large bobbins, are fed out from the back of the mule by a pair of rollers. The spindles are on a carriage which moves away from these rollers at the beginning of the cycle, inserting just enough twist to prevent the slubbing from breaking. When the carriage has moved out about 4 ft the delivery rollers stop, so that the fibres are now being drafted (i.e. the slubbing is attenuated). The carriage moves out about another 2 ft and stops. The speed of the spindles increases, inserting the required amount of twist in the slubbing (the spindles are slightly inclined from the vertical towards the delivery roller end so that at each turn of the spindle the slubbing slips off the spindle point and a turn of twist is inserted). At this stage the carriage moves in a few inches to allow for the tightening of the yarn (as it may now be termed) with the increasing twist. When the required amount of twist has been inserted, the direction of rotation of the spindles reverses so as to unwind the few turns of yarn coiling up to the spindle point. The carriage then moves in towards the rollers, the spindles now rotating in the original direction to wind on the yarn. During all this time two stout wires (faller and counter-faller) control the yarn so that it is wound on to the cop on the spindle to form a suitable package. It will be appreciated that a remarkable co-ordination of all the working parts is required to achieve this result satisfactorily and automatically—and astonishing that the basic principle was devised by Roberts in 1825.

The action of the mule is thus intermittent: it spins only on the outward run, winding the yarn on the cop during the inward run. This, and the large amount of floor space it takes up, are disadvantages; in addition the mechanism is necessarily complicated, calling for more expert maintenance and "tuning" than is demanded by the ring frame.

The woollen ring spinning frame is somewhat similar to its worsted counterpart (see p. 139), and is thus continuous in action. There is no drafting of the fibres between rollers, however. The drafting takes place between a pair of delivery rollers and the spindle unit, a variety of devices being used to control this drafting action and to prevent the thread from drafting apart; this control is usually achieved by the insertion of temporary twist. Many new types of ring frame have been introduced since the Second World War by British and foreign textile machinery makers.

The details of spinning machines must be sought in other books; the present intention is to stress the main differences between a worsted and a woollen yarn, and the principal way in which these differences are brought about. In worsted spinning the fibres are given their final drafting between two pairs of rollers (roller drafting) so that they remain smooth and parallel in the yarn; the required amount of twist is then inserted by the spindle unit. In woollen spinning the drafting and twisting take place at the same time ("drafting against twist"); this results in the longer fibres taking most of the strain while the shorter ones find their way to the outside, their ends protruding to make a fuzzier and "fuller", "loftier" yarn. The student is recommended to read Morton and Wray (see p. 145) to gain fuller understanding of this subject, and Brearley (see p. 130) for up-to-date descriptions of the machinery.

Twisting, Winding, Reeling, and Warping

Several other processes are necessary before either worsted or woollen yarn is ready for weaving, machine knitting, or hand knitting. Single yarn is sometimes used in weaving, particularly for weft, but as a rule two or more yarns are twisted together on a frame of the ring or cap type without drafting rollers. This operation is known as twisting or folding, and the resultant yarns are sometimes referred to as "plied". The twisting together of two or more plied yarns is known as cabling.

In addition, the different processes following spinning or twisting demand yarn wound as different forms of package, and so the yarn has to be rewound on special machines.

The bobbin or tube on to which yarn is wound in spinning is not suitable for mounting in the shuttle for weaving. The yarn is therefore rewound on to a pirn, a package suitable for that purpose.

For warping (see below) and for machine knitting, long lengths of yarn are required, and it is wound either into a cylindrical "cheese" or a cone, the lengths of yarn from the spinning package being knotted together by an automatic hand knotter (or joined together by an adhesive—a method developed by Wira).

For yarn dyeing or scouring the spinning packages may be reeled into hanks; hand knitting yarn is also reeled. Several reeled hanks are bunched together and these are made up into bundles.

The warp threads for weaving, may be several thousand, have to be arranged in the right order, cut to the right length and wound with even tension, on to the "weaver's beam" at the back of the loom. The operation starts, away from the loom, by placing cheeses or cones of yarn on to a creel, from which they are wound on to a large cylinder, and cut. From this cylinder they can be wound on to the weaver's beam.

Some Literature on Worsted and Woollen Yarn Manufacture

BEEVERS, H., *Practical Spinning on the Bradford System*, Heywood (Textile Machinery Series) 1964 (first printed 1954). Suitable for students. The author, after serving on the staff of the Wool Industries Research Association, was a lecturer at Bradford Technical College, and subsequently Head of the Textile Department of Keighley Technical College.

BEEVERS, H., *The Practice of Bradford Open Drawing*, Heywood (Textile Machinery Series), 1964 (first printed 1954). Suitable for students. Written in lucid style, calculations being simply explained.

BREARLEY, A. (see p. 130).

GEE, N. C., *Shoddy and Mungo Manufacture*, Emmott & Co., 1950. An important book, the literature in this field being sparse. The author was Head of the Textile Department of Dewsbury Technical College.

GRIFFIN, T. F., *Practical Worsted Carding*, Heywood (Textile Machinery Series), 1963 (first printed 1957). A useful book covering sorting, blending, shaking, scouring, and drying, as well as carding, by an author with industrial and teaching (university) experience.

GRIFFIN, T. F., *Practical Worsted Combing*, National Trade Press (Textile Machinery Series), 1953. Some knowledge of combing is assumed. The operation and maintenance of backwashing and gilling machines, and Noble and rectilinear combs is explained.

MACKERETH, L., *Woollen Carding and Spinning*, Wool Review Ltd., 1967. Explains machinery and the way it works. Useful for students taking City and Guilds craft course; useful also in the factory.

MORTON, W. E., and WRAY, G. R., *An Introduction to the Study of Spinning*, Longmans, 3rd edn., 1962. A standard book for students and most interesting for anybody to read. In the first part raw materials are described; in the second part the fundamentals of spinning and the preparatory processes are admirably explained.

NEEDHAM, H., *Practical Drawing and Spinning on the Continental System*, Heywood (Textile Machinery Series), 1955. Good practical information for students and others by an author with both industrial and technical college teaching experience.

International Wool Secretariat Articles

The following articles in the International Wool Secretariat's series, *Wool Science Review*, are intended mainly for the textile scientist and technologist:

MARTINDALE, J. G., Woollen spinning on the mule, No. 16, p. 3, Nov. 1956.

THORNDIKE, G. H., Woollen ring frame spinning, No. 17, p. 3, July 1957.

ANDERSON, S. L., Neps in worsted slivers—origin, constitution, and estimation, No. 22, p. 28, March 1963.

MONFORT, F., GRIGNET, J., and BRENY, H. Regularity of tops, slivers and yarns, Part 1, No. 24, p. 49, Feb. 1964; Part 2, No. 25, p. 32, Sept. 1964; Part 3, No. 26, p. 37, Dec. 1964.

BRACH, J., and BIELEN, R., Carbonising: a survey of recent research in Belgium, No. 25, p. 45, Sept. 1964.

PRESSLEY, T. A., and CREWTHER, W. G., Carbonising: recent research in Australia, No. 26, p. 25, Dec. 1964.

ONIONS, W. J., The hairiness of wool yarns, No. 27, p. 35, Aug. 1965.

WOOD, G. F., Solvent scouring of raw wool, No. 23, p. 40, July 1963.

GRIGNET, J., Controlling and removing thickness faults in yarns, Part 1, No. 33, p. 31, Oct. 1967.

WEAVING

Before weaving can be started, the warp threads have to be drawn through the eyes of wires (or steel strips or cords) in a set of healds, which are raised and lowered automatically during weaving according to the requirements of the cloth's pattern. This is done in a framework away from the loom so that productive time is not wasted. One operative, the drawer-in, puts a hook (somewhat similar to a crochet hook) through each heald eye in turn, and another operator—the reacher-in—places the correct thread into it from the weaver's beam which is mounted on that side of the framework. An automatic device, the Wira Reaching-in machine, has been invented by Wira to take the place of the reacher-in. When the piece to be woven has the same warp arrangement ("draft") as the previous piece, the process of drawing-in is not necessary: the new warp threads are knotted, by hand or machine, to the old threads and drawn through by them.

Many looms are fitted with an automatic device for stopping the loom when a warp thread breaks, thus enabling the loom minder to rectify the matter before a long fault develops. This warp-stop motion requires a small, metal "dropper" to be placed on each thread, this being done by hand or by means of a machine such as the Wira Dropper Pinning Machine.

There are many types of loom and methods of weaving, so the process can be touched on only very superficially in this book.

The basic operations of weaving are (a) the raising and lowering of the healds to form a "shed" for the weft thread to pass through,

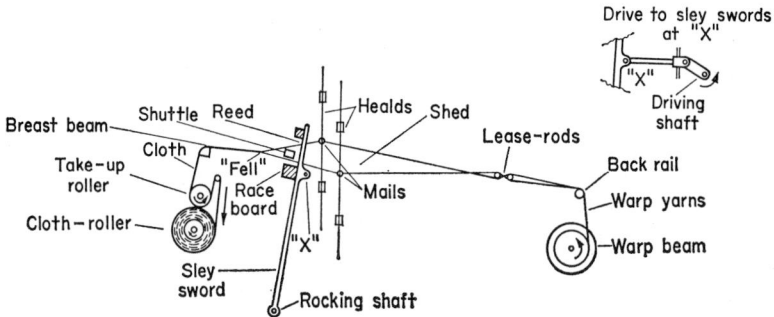

FIG. 7. Simplified diagram of loom, illustrating principles. (From *Worsted* by Alan Brearley, Pitman.)

(b) the passing of the weft thread through the shed, (c) the beating-up of each weft thread. As weaving proceeds, the warp beam is allowed to rotate under the control of a let-off motion, whose action may be frictional or positive. At the same time, a roller at the front of the loom winds on the woven cloth, its speed being regulated by the number of picks (weft threads) per inch (Fig. 7).

The healds are raised and lowered by a mechanism designed for the particular type of loom (see below). After the shuttle has passed through the shed, it is beaten up against the previous one by the reed, the vertical wires of which also keep the warp threads in their proper position. To prevent the cloth being bowed in by the weft tension the selvedges are held by a revolving grip of the pin or pincer type, or the cloth is controlled by the Wira Full-width Temple.

There are three main types of loom: Tappet, Dobby, and Jacquard. In a Tappet loom the passage of the weft ("picking") is controlled by a tappet motion which allows only simple designs. The mechanism of the Dobby can control a large number of heald shafts and allows for more complicated patterns. The Jacquard mechanism, controlled by a punched-card device, enables such patterns as floral designs to be woven.

The operation of all machine looms is automatic, but the term automatic loom is now applied to one that has a device for changing either the shuttle or the pirn in the shuttle when the weft yarn is expended, whereas in non-automatic looms the operative has to do this.

New principles are being introduced into the weaving process, particularly for inserting the weft thread, keeping the loom automatically supplied with weft, and for increasing weaving speed. The word "loom", stemming as it does from the Anglo-Saxon *geloma*, signifying a household implement (cf. heirloom), would seem to be no longer appropriate to the modern "weaving machine". In appearance, these new machines are more streamlined and have less tophamper.

The new methods of inserting the weft are designed to get away from the mechanically inefficient operation of throwing a heavy shuttle through the shed, only to stop and return it. Amongst the improved devices are the bullet, rapier, and jet. In all of these the weft supply is sited at the side of the machine, only sufficient for one pick being taken through the shed. In the bullet type a succession of small carriers take successive picks through the shed, returning by a lower level for more weft. In the rapier or gripper type (the principle of which, incidentally, was invented in the seventeenth century by a French naval officer!) the weft is taken by a pincer-like device from the side of the machine to the centre of the shed, where a similar device takes the weft for the completion of the pick. In jet looms the weft is blown through the shed by a jet of air; for some other fibres a jet of water is used, but this has disadvantages for wool, which readily absorbs moisture.

Burling and Mending

After weaving, the piece is examined, the main faults requiring attention being marked with chalk. The two operations done at this stage are known as burling and mending, the latter being the more expert job.

In burling, slubs (thick places in the yarn), neps (small clusters of fibre), and any extraneous matter are removed, and knots may be worked through from the face to the back of the cloth.

In mending, appropriate lengths of yarn are sewn in, according to the design, to replace incorrect ones or long slubs.

Some Literature on Weaving

The following four books give up-to-date information on modern looms:

AITKEN, J. B., *Automatic Weaving*, Columbine Press, 1965. Much of this book is on the preparation of warp and weft for weaving, but automatic looms are described in two of the chapters.

DUXBURY, V., and WRAY, G. R., (Eds.), *Modern Developments in Weaving Machinery*, Columbine Press, 1962. For the textile scientist and technologist and advanced students.

FOSTER, R., *Positive Let-off Motions*, Wool Industries Research Association, 1961. One of the objects of this book is to help the loom tuner to understand the principles on which positive let-off motions work, so that they may use and maintain them to the best advantage. An excellent book, too, for students.

BRITISH NORTHROP LTD., *Automatic Weaving: the northrop system*, 1962.

International Wool Secretariat Articles

The following articles in the International Wool Secretariat's series, *Wool Science Review*, are intended mainly for the textile scientist and technologist.

> TOWNSEND, M., The scientist looks at the wool industry: weaving, Part 1, No. 18, p. 5, Oct. 1960; Part 2, No. 19, p. 3, June 1961; Part 3, No. 20, p. 3, Dec. 1961; Part 4, No. 21, p. 3, Aug. 1962.

Wool Industries Research Association Leaflets

The Wool Industries Research Association has developed many processing accessories, some of which—such as the following three—are in commercial production. Illustrated leaflets giving brief descriptions and names of makers are available to bona fide inquirers. The name of each device is prefixed by the term Wira.

  (i) Reaching-in Machine. Enables warp threads to be drawn in preparatory to weaving, without the assistance of a reacher-in (a junior operative).
 (ii) Dropper Pinning Machine. Places on warp threads the pins required by the warp stop motion.
(iii) Full-width Temple. Reduces considerably the breakage of warp threads in the weaving of many types of cloth.

DYEING AND FINISHING

The Finishing of Worsted and Woollen Cloths

A piece of cloth straight from the loom is usually dirty and harsh in handle. The work of the designer and the processors up to and including weaving are embodied in it, but it is the job of the dyers and finishers to impart the desired handle, colour, and general appearance, which make the cloth a saleable product in a competitive world market. In the woollen section of the industry all of this may be done by the firm that has processed the cloth for raw wool; but the dyeing may be done on commission for woollen manufacturers who have their own finishing plants. Most worsteds (particularly fine worsteds), however, are handled by commission dyers and finishers.

No hard-and-fast rules can be laid down for the finishing routine of a cloth: that for a worsted is different from that for a woollen cloth, and within those differences individual firms have their own preferences.

Piece scouring is usually the first process, the cloth being treated with a liquor containing soap or a synthetic detergent), sodium carbonate (or some other alkali), and water. Some cloths are given a preliminary setting treatment before scouring, to prevent subsequent distortion; this is done by crabbing, the cloth being wound around a roller and passed through hot water; alternatively, it may have steam blown through it while wet, this being known as steaming or wet blowing.

Milling (basically the same as the old fulling process) is typically a woollen treatment, though some worsteds may be slightly milled. Modern milling machines have a rotary action and squeeze rollers for felting the cloth, but the heavy wooden hammer type is still sometimes used.

Before further finishing, as much water as possible is removed by a hydro-extractor ("wuzzer"), and the cloth is dried by hot air and slightly stretched in a tenter to remove creases.

Either worsteds or woollens may be dyed at this stage (see next section).

Raising the surface fibres on a fine West of England woollen cloth is still done on a teasel gig, but for most woollens a card wire raising machine is used for the same purpose; in the United States this is known as napping. In another process the cloth is drawn over a plush fabric to produce the required napped surface. Whether a cloth is raised or not, it is usually cropped in a machine working on the same principle as an ordinary lawn mower to tidy the surface.

Other processes are dry blowing in which steam is blown through the cloth whilst it is on a roller, pressing, and potting (or boiling) in which it is immersed in a very dilute acid solution. In addition, woollen cloth may be carbonized if this was not done after raw wool scouring.

Finally, some cloths such as suitings are subjected to London Shrinking, in which they are slightly damped and allowed to dry while there is no tension in them. This is designed to release any strains that may still be in the cloth after all the manufacturing processes, and thus prevent a garment from shrinking when being pressed or in wear.

Dyeing

Natural wool has a yellowish tinge so, before dyeing, its white-ness may be improved by bleaching at some convenient stage as raw wool, sliver, top, yarn, or fabric. Sulphur stoving is still sometimes used, but this does not have a permanent effect, so hydrogen peroxide treatment is preferred.

Many books on dyeing cover the other fibres as well as wool, so care should be taken to check that any particular information on dyes, methods, and machinery does apply to wool. It must be added, however, that wool has an affinity for nearly all dyestuffs. A recent book specifically on wool dyeing is that by Bird (see p. 154).

There are five main types of dyes used for wool: acid dyes, mordant dyes, metal complex dyes, vat dyes, and natural dyes.

Acid dyes are of two kinds—levelling and milling. Levelling acid dyes are popular, being convenient to use in a wide range of colours; as the name implies, they give good level results, and an additional advantage is that several dyes of this kind can be used together to give the desired shade. Their light-fastness is good, but not their wet-fastness. Milling acid dyes do not give such bright colours, but their wet-fastness is good; they are therefore used on fabrics that are to be given a milling or other wet treatment subsequently, and for which good fastness to wash-ing is desirable.

Mordant dyes are those that require combining with a metal, usually some form of chrome such as potassium dichromate, to make them combine satisfactorily with the wool substance. The mordant may be applied before the dyestuff (chrome mordant process), at the same time as the dyestuff (metachrome process), or after it (afterchrome process). Mordant dyes have good fastness both to light and to washing.

Metal complex dyes enable mordant dyeing to be done somewhat more conveniently; their fastness to washing is very good, and the method facilitates matching because more dyestuff can be added and the effect gauged during processing.

Vat dyeing for wool is virtually restricted to the use of indigo, and is much less used than it was in the past; the method is complicated, but gives good results for fastness to light and washing, and is sometimes favoured for piece dyeing usually in combination with chrome or milling acid colours.

Natural dyes still in use for wool are cochineal and logwood. A tin mordant is used with cochineal to give scarlet and a chrome mordant with logwood for dark blues and blacks. Another natural dye still used for special purposes, sometimes in combination with logwood, is fustic.

In the manufacture of worsted yarn and cloth, dyeing is never done before combing. After combing and subsequent gilling (see p. 135) the worsted sliver may be dyed in the form of balls of top (top dyeing), or in hanks (slubbing dyeing). Dyeing at this stage enables colour blending to be incorporated in the subsequent drawing. Yarn is usually dyed in cheese form (see p. 144), the liquor being passed through the cheese in both directions while it is mounted on a perforated spindle. Whereas in top, slubbing, and yarn dyeing the liquor is passed through the material, in piece dyeing the practice is reversed because the cloth, several pieces joined end to end, can conveniently be circulated through the dyebath.

In the manufacture of woollen yarn and cloth raw wool may be dyed, the desired shade being achieved by means of blending, and thorough mixing in carding. Thus a grey shade may be obtained by blending blue, red, white, and black wool before carding. Shoddy and mungo are usually dyed, or stripped and re-dyed, before blending.

Printing

The three principal methods of printing are known as direct style, discharge style, and resist style. In the direct style the pattern is printed on to white cloth, or on to a coloured one (over-printing). In the discharge style a white or near-white pattern is produced on a coloured cloth by printing with a substance that destroys the ground shade already on the cloth. The principle of the resist style is first to print the desired pattern on a cloth with a substance that will prevent dye being absorbed by the wool; the cloth is then dyed.

Some Literature on Finishing, Dyeing, and Printing

There is a great deal of literature on these topics; the following list and accompanying remarks are therefore to a certain extent personally selective.

Processing

BIRD, C. L., *The Theory and Practice of Wool Dyeing*, Society of Dyers and Colourists, 3rd edn., 1963. The subjects dealt with are: dyeing in relation to other textile processes; theory of wool dyeing; wet treatments associated with dyeing; acid, metal-complex, chrome, and indigo dyes; union dyeing, recent developments in wool dyeing; levelling and stripping; water and auxiliary products; machinery for dyeing wool. Three appendixes give information on fastness requirements, acidity and alkalinity, and manufacturers of dyestuffs, auxiliary products, and machinery.

BLACKSHAW, H., and BRIGHTMAN, R., *Dictionary of Dyeing and Textile Printing*, Newnes, 1961. As well as a glossary of technical terms there is a long reading list.

CHEETHAM, R. C., *Dyeing Fibre Blends*, D. Van Nostrand Co., 1966. Much of this book is on man-made fibres, but wool in blends is also discussed.

COCKETT, S. R., *Dyeing and Printing*, Pitman (Common Commodities and Industries Series), 1964. A good general account in not-too-technical language, useful for students, people in other sections of the industry, and anyone interested in the subject.

HALL, A. J., *A Handbook of Textile Dyeing and Printing*, National Trade Press, 1955. Dyes, methods, and machinery are included for the various fibres for dyeing at all stages of manufacture, and for printing. The fastness of dyed and printed fabric, and other topics, are included. As with the author's other books, the writing is clear and not too technical.

HALL, A. J., *Textile Finishing*, Heywood, 3rd edn., 1966. A general account suitable for both students and technologists.

LAWRIE, L. G., *A Bibliography of Dyeing and Textile Printing*, Chapman & Hall, 1949. Brief particulars of over 800 books dating from the sixteenth century onwards.

MARSH, J. T., *An Introduction to Textile Bleaching*, Chapman & Hall, 4th (revised) impression, 1956. This is a major work covering much more than the actual bleaching process; sections are included on raw wool, yarn and piece scouring, carbonizing, milling, and crabbing.

MARSH, J. T., *An Introduction to Textile Finishing*, Chapman & Hall, 2nd edn., 1966. A major work by a well-known textile chemist. There is plenty of up-to-date information on wool processing, including: finishing machines, crêping, formaldehyde treatment (as a protective agent in alkaline wet processes and for other purposes), permanent set, milling, non-felting treatments, mothproofing, and mildewproofing.

TROTMAN, E. R., *Dyeing and Chemical Technology of Textile Fibres*, Griffin, 3rd edn., 1964. This is the third, rewritten and enlarged, edition of *Bleaching, Dyeing and Chemical Technology of Textile Fibres*. It is a major work and, in addition to the dyeing of wool, covers water purification, detergents and scouring, bleaching, shrink-proof finishes, and the theory of colour. The book is suitable for the man in the industry, the technologist, and the advanced student.

BRITISH COLOUR COUNCIL, *Dictionary of Colour Standards*, 2nd edn., 1951. The colours and their names are those widely known and accepted in industry; they are shown on silk ribbon woven to show each colour in gloss and matt finish. A companion volume gives the history of each colour. The *Dictionary*, showing the same range of 240 colours in wool yarn, is available without the history volume.

ICI DYESTUFFS DIVISION, *An Introduction to Textile Printing*, Butterworths, 2nd edn., 1967. A practical book for students.

Index to Textile Auxiliaries, published by Harlequin Press for the International Dyer, 1967. Classified in three main sections: (i) alphabetical, descriptive list of textile auxiliaries, (ii) products under their uses, (iii) names, addresses, etc., of producers.

International Wool Secretariat Articles

The following articles in the International Wool Secretariat's series, *Wool Science Review*, are intended mainly for the textile scientist and technologist.

STEVENS, C. B., Dyeing resist processes for wool, No. 15, p. 13, March 1956.

STEVENS, C. B., Cross dyeing all-wool fabrics, No. 16, p. 15, Nov. 1956.

MOXON, B. F. J., Problems and progress in woollen and worsted piece scouring, No. 23, p. 13, July 1963.

PRESTON, J. M., The dyeing of wool: current practice and recent research. Part 1, The nature of wool fibres and of wool dyes, No. 30, p. 1, Aug. 1966; Part 2, The dyeing of wool, No. 31, p. 32, Jan. 1967; Part 3, Colour theory and dyeing practice, No. 32, p. 36, July 1967.

CHESNER, L., Wool bleaching, Part 1, No. 30, p. 16, Aug. 1966; Part 2, No. 31, p. 1, Jan. 1967.

BAIRD, K., Hygral expansion in wool fabrics, No. 31, p. 12, Jan. 1967.

ANON, Wool stretch fabrics, No. 31, p. 40, Jan. 1967.

Textile Chemistry

Many of the above books include sections on textile chemistry, or the subject is embodied in the text; the following books are more directly concerned with textile chemistry applying to dyeing, printing, and finishing:

COCKETT, S. R., and HILTON, K. A., *Basic Chemistry of Textile Colouring and Finishing*, National Trade Press, 1955. This, and the companion volume below by the same authors, provide information on basic textile chemistry suitable for both students and those in the industry.

COCKETT, S. R., and HILTON, K. A., *Basic Chemistry of Textile Preparation*, National Trade Press, 1955. (See above.)

DISEREUS, L., *Chemical Technology of Dyeing and Printing* (2 vols.), Reinhold, New York, 1948, and Chapman & Hall, 1951.

VICKERSTAFF, T., *The Physical Chemistry of Dyeing*, Oliver & Boyd, 2nd edn., 1954. This book, sponsored by ICI Ltd., is a valuable work for the advanced student, technologist, and scientist.

NON-WOVEN FABRICS

Woven woollen cloth may be given a heavy felting treatment in finishing, the pattern of warp and weft threads being no longer discernible; this is known as woven felt. In another type of felt manufacture the material is neither woven nor spun: the fibres are consolidated into a firm fabric by means of pressure, rubbing, moisture, and heat; this material is known as pressed felt.

Many different qualities of pressed felt are used for a variety of end products ranging from surgical pads to mechanical mouldings; the precise method of manufacture also varies accordingly, and the following brief description is therefore very general. The

raw material is blended, opened, and carded into a web, many
layers being laid on top of each other to form a "batt", which is
subjected to pressure and rubbing, whilst moist, on either a
flat, or roller hardening machine. After hardening, the material
may be further treated in the falling hammer type of fulling
stocks or in a similar machine known as a bumper. The felt is
finally finished by treatments that vary according to the end use.

In a modern form of non-woven fabric fibres are bonded together. Some special man-made fibre, one that can readily be
softened into a tacky condition, is evenly distributed throughout
wool or other fibres, and the blend in the form of a thick web is
hot pressed so that the special fibres melt and bond the whole into
a felt-like fabric.

There is also a process in which felting and sewing are combined.

Some Literature on Non-woven Fabrics

The following article in the International Wool Secretariat's
series, *Wool Science Review*, gives a not-too-technical account
of the manufacture of pressed felt.

> BARR, T., The manufacture of pressed felts, No. 26, p. 15,
> Dec. 1964.

Information on modern non-woven fabrics will be found in
technical journals, and in some general books such as Hall's
The Standard Handbook of Textiles (see p. 131). A useful
book on the subject published in the United States is:

> BURESH, F. M., *Nonwoven Fabrics*, Reinhold, 1962.

SPECIAL FINISHING TREATMENTS

There are today many new treatments devised by the textile
scientist for giving wool yarn and fabrics desirable properties
additional to those inherent in the natural fibre. These, which are
often referred to as "Easy-Care" properties, include shrink
resistance, durable pleating and creasing, flat setting, mothproofing, showerproofing, and stainproofing.

There are two main types of shrinkage in woven and knitted fabrics: relaxation and felting. During manufacture, the yarn and the cloth are subjected to strains, sometimes whilst damp, and these become temporarily set in the cloth, which thus tends to relax when it is no longer under any tension. If nothing were done about this, a suit might shrink during wear, for example in a shower of rain. The object of London Shrinking (see p. 152) and similar processes is to prevent this relaxation shrinkage taking place in a suit; it therefore no longer concerns us in this section.

The property of felting is a unique advantage of the wool fibre; heavy felting is essential in such cloths as melton, and there is some degree of felting in the finishing treatment of all woollen cloths; some worsteds, too, are enhanced by a slight felting effect which gives that typical warm handle unique to wool. Felting during washing and in wear, however, is obviously undesirable; so this aspect has been a subject of research for many years. In the natural state the tendency of wool fibres is to get into a huddle from which they cannot extricate themselves; this is partly due to the overlapping scaly surface, and research has revealed also an effect arising from the fine structure of the fibre surface. Most commercial methods for conferring shrink resistance are therefore designed to modify the fibre surface so that there is no longer a tendency for fibres to migrate in one direction preferentially (that of the root end); this tendency is known as DFE (differential frictional effect).

In early methods, a wet chlorination treatment was used (Fig. 8) but adequate control was impossible because of the marked affinity of wool for chlorine in the presence of water. The Wool Industries Research Association therefore devised a dry chlorination process, the material being subjected to gaseous chlorine in an autoclave. The practical advantages of wet treatment subsequently led to the invention of many methods on these lines that can be adequately controlled. In a later process devised by Wira a dilute solution of peracetic acid and sodium hypochlorite is used; in addition to good control this process gives the wool a

soft handle and good white colour. There are now many satisfactory methods for producing shrink-resist wool. The Stevenson
XC process uses first a dilute solution of permonosulphuric acid
followed by immersion in a solution containing sodium sulphite
(a reducing agent). In the Melafix processes wool is treated with
an acidified solution of sodium hypochlorite in the presence of
melamine formaldehyde resins, and this gives a very even treatment. The International Wool Secretariat treatment, IWS-7, in

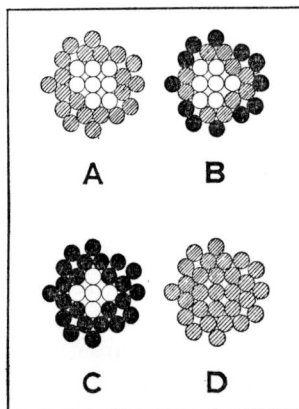

FIG. 8. Shrink-resistant wool. Cross-sections of yarns show uneven
and even (D) treatment of fibres. (From *An Introduction to Textile
Finishing* by J. T. Marsh, Chapman & Hall).

which wool is treated with a solution of potassium permanganate
in a saturated solution of Glauber's salt at a low temperature, gives
excellent shrink resistance and a soft handle, making it eminently
suitable for knitwear. In a more recent IWS process launched in
1966, known as DCCA (dichloroisocyanuric acid), wool tops
(see p. 135) are run through a bath of the acid on the production
line. During 1966 the process was tried out in mills in several
countries and proved to be satisfactory. In addition to the
continuous process for tops, DCCA is used commercially in batch

applications at various stages of manufacture for yarns, blankets, piece goods, and garments.

Other modern treatments are used to produce durable creases in trousers and pleats in skirts. The basic principle is to set the cloth in the desired formation, so it can be used also for imparting a flat setting. For creases, pleats, and flat setting, the processes can be regarded as durable because the set imparted will remain until the garment is subjected to more severe relaxation conditions ("unsetting" so to speak) in washing or in wear—and this would not normally occur. In a Wira process a steaming treatment is used without any chemicals, which can be a great advantage; it can be applied to a wide range of fabrics including worsted suitings, woollen tweeds, and all-wool knitted jersey fabric. In the Immacula process, developed originally at Leeds University (inquiries regarding this patented process should now be addressed to Proban Ltd., Manchester), disulphite bonds of the wool molecule are broken and rebuilt so that the fibres and the fabric are in the desired formation. The fabric can be sprayed with sodium bisulphite solution immediately before pressing to give a very sharp and durable crease; alternatively, the moistened, impregnated, and dried fabric can be pressed, this being preferred as a commercial process because the tailor has only to damp the fabric before pressing. The Si-ro-set process, invented in Australia by the Commonwealth Scientific and Industrial Research Organization (CSIRO) uses ammonium thioglycollate, but this chemical has largely been replaced by one known as MEAS (monoethanolamine sesquisulphite), and the process has become known in Great Britain as IWS-4. In this process an aqueous solution of MEAS can be applied either to the cloth before it is made into a garment, or to garments, by spray apparatus or aerosol package. This makes the durable creasing or pleating process very convenient to use.

The prevention of damage to wool by moth grubs is today both easy and cheap. Many methods have been used with varying degrees of success, but really satisfactory mothproofing agents were not achieved until the 1920's when organic compounds become available which have a similar affinity for wool as that of a dye. These can be applied in many ways and for particular purposes; some are used cheaply and conveniently in the dyebath so that mothproofing does not entail an additional wet process. Some of the agents are in fact colourless dyes. One modern approach is to bring about a fundamental and permanent change in the chemical structure of the wool fibre, and this can be done in such a way that the natural and desirable properties of wool are not adversely affected. The broad principle of this type of method is to introduce into a part of the molecular structure of the wool fibre chemical groups that make the wool substance indigestible to the moth grub. This line of research has been given impetus by the argument that the use of certain compounds of the insecticide type could have toxic effects on humans, and could have ill effects following constant contact with a fabric treated with such substances. However, at present (1967) all of the many effective mothproofing agents contain compounds that could theoretically be harmful to humans if used in sufficient quantities. But their use is under strict control, and the effects of existing and newly introduced agents are kept under observation. The dangers are virtually non-existent in view of the small concentrations that are required. For example, Dieldrin, now widely used, is applied at a concentration of 500 parts per million of wool.

Showerproofing by means of wax is an old method, and some modern methods still use an emulsion of wax and metallic salt, but they are not as a rule fast to washing or dry cleaning. More permanent fastness is now obtained by the new silicone finishes. The structure of the fabric is important, gabardine for raincoats being one of the most common; but many other types of wool fabrics, including woollens, can now be rendered showerproof. It must be stressed that there is a definite distinction between showerproofing and waterproofing. A fabric can be made completely waterproof by such treatments as rubberizing and coating with a plastic; but this is not generally desirable in clothing because it prevents water vapour from passing outwards from the body. Raindrops run off a showerproofed fabric, which still, however, remains porous to water vapour and air.

Stainproofing also can be conferred by modern methods of showerproofing, but a wax treatment is not proof to oil or grease. Mystolene MK3 used in conjunction with fluorcarbon compounds repels oil and grease as well as aqueous stains, and another similar finish is Scotchgard. The Newsome process is used by the woollen manufacturing firm of that name for their own cloths.

Some Literature on Special Finishing Treatments

Many of the general books on textile processing, and, of course, those on finishing, have sections on special finishing treatments, but the following are specifically concerned with the subject:

MOILLIET, J. W. (Ed.), *Waterproofing and Water-repellency*, Elsevier, 1963. Covers a wide field, including the waterproofing of paper and building materials, but there are sections on the proofing of textiles, testing, and scientific background.

MONCRIEFF, R. W., *Mothproofing*, Leonard Hill, 1950. A not-too-technical account of moths, damage, proofing and testing.

MONCRIEFF, R. W., *Wool Shrinkage and its Prevention*, National Trade Press, 1953. Deals thoroughly with relaxation and felting shrinkage, and the processes in use at that time or proposed, and with testing.

MOSS, A. J. E., *Stain Removal: the technique of spotting*, Trader Publishing Co. (for "Power Laundry"), 1950.

MOSS, A. J. E., *Clothes Care*, Heywood, 1961.

SPEEL, H. C., and SCHWARZ, E. W. K. (Eds.) *Textile Chemicals and Auxiliaries, with Special Reference to Surfactants and Finishes*, Reinhold, 2nd edn., 1957.

WEST, T. P., and CAMPBELL, G. A., *DDT and Newer Persistent Insecticides*, Chapman & Hall, 2nd edn., 1950.

Buyers' Guide to DYLAN Washable Wool, Precision Processes (Textiles) Ltd., Ambergate, 1967. Separate United Kingdom and Overseas editions.

Dylan Shrink-resistant Wool Yarns, Precision Processes (Textiles) Ltd., Ambergate, 1967. A useful guide to types and sources of shrink-resistant wool yarns.

International Wool Secretariat Literature

The three IWS booklets explain special finishes simply yet authoritatively, and list the sources from which further information can be obtained:

(a) *Easy Washability.*
(b) *Durable Pleating, Creasing, and Flat Setting.*
(c) *Mothproofing, Showerproofing, and Stainproofing.*

The following articles in the International Wool Secretariat's series, *Wool Science Review*, are intended mainly for the textile scientist and technologist:

ANON., A new process for compacting textile materials, No. 17, p. 50, July 1957.

ANON., Shrink-resist processes for Wool, Part 1, The factors that affect felting shrinkage, No. 17, p. 16, July 1957; Part 2, Commercial methods, No. 18, p. 18, Oct. 1960.

ANON., The sterilization of wool blankets, Part 1, No. 19, p. 46, June 1961; Part 2, No. 20, p. 45, Dec. 1961.

MAKINSON, K. R., Felting: the present picture; recent observations on the mechanism of felting, No. 24, p. 34, Feb. 1964.

FARNWORTH, A., Principles and industrial applications of permanent wool setting. Part 1, Principles involved, No. 24, p. 1, Feb. 1964; Part 2, Industrial Applications, No. 25, p. 17, Sept. 1964.

WASLEY, W. L., WHITFIELD, R. E., and MILLER, L. A., Interfacial graft polymerization as a treatment for wool, No. 26, p. 1, Dec. 1964.

McPHEE, J. R., The present situation in the mothproofing of wool. Part 1, No. 27, p. 1, Aug. 1965; Part 2, No. 28, p. 33, Nov. 1965.

ABBOTT, N. J., Wrinkle resistance in wool fabrics. No. 32, p. 23, 1967.

MEASUREMENT, TESTING, AND CONTROL

The modern wool textile industry employs methods of testing and control at every stage of manufacture. The development of the methods of test and equipment represents the work of many different types of research worker. The requirement for a new testing technique has sometimes arisen in the laboratories of Wira, and when the problem has been satisfactorily solved arrangements are as a rule made with a firm of instrument makers for the commercial production of a device suitable for use in industry (see p. 113).

Another subject that has received much attention by Wira is sampling; the full value of good testing and control methods will not be achieved unless the samples taken for testing are truly representative of the bulk about which information is required. Sampling methods for wool at various stages of manufacture have therefore been devised. Statistical reasoning has to be used at every stage of testing, both in deciding the number of specimens to be tested and the way in which the results should be analysed.

Space does not permit the mention of all the types of testing and testing instruments that are used in the industry today, but the following brief account indicates that there is scope for many kinds of scientific and technological skill both in the research laboratory and in the testing and quality control departments of factories.

Raw wool, and indeed wool at the various stages of processing, contains a certain amount of moisture, so this has to be measured accurately for the purposes of both processing and accounting. Moisture content is normally calculated as a percentage of the dry weight and is known as "regain". Raw wool before processing contains grease, vegetable matter, soil, and other matter; the proportion of actual wool can be determined by scouring trials on large samples, but commercially suitable methods now exist for analysing raw wool by means of core testing.

Single fibres are tested for extension, elasticity, and recovery from extension under various conditions, measurements being also made of length, fineness, and crimp (the natural waviness of the fibre). Diameter or fineness (the wool fibre is slightly elliptical) is an important property in processing, so methods have been devised for determining within a few minutes the average fineness of a sample of fibres. Fibre length, another important property, can be investigated thoroughly by modern methods; in worsted drawing and spinning, not only the average length of the fibres being processed, but also the numerical proportions of the various lengths, can be shown diagrammatically.

Sliver and yarn testing, particularly for irregularity of thickness along the length, assumed a new importance with the introduction of modern methods of worsted drawing and spinning, which demand a greater degree of accuracy in machine setting. The variations of irregularity are both random and periodic, and of short- and long-term variation, and these have to be studied with regard to their deviation from the mean, which involves such statistical conceptions as variance, standard deviation, and co-efficient of variation. Yarns are also tested for strength in many different types of machine, standard lengths being extended to break, and the results being recorded automatically. Woollen yarns can be controlled during production for thickness along the length by means of the Wira Autocount, which exercises an automatic control over the thickness of the carded web being produced by the carding machine for spinning into woollen yarn.

Quite apart from irregularity the size or fineness of worsted and woollen yarns has to be measured, this being known as the count, or linear density. Traditionally there have been many different yarn counting systems, those in the wool textile industry being based on the length of a given weight of yarn. Thus in one pound of a 48s worsted yarn there are $48 \times 560 = 26,880$ yards; and in one pound of 20s Yorkshire Skeins Woollen (YSW) there are $20 \times 256 = 5120$ yards. In order to simplify transactions between different industries and different countries, the International Standards Organization evolved a universal count system known as the Tex system. This system is based on weight per length instead of length per weight, and so has the advantage that as yarn thickness increases, the Tex value increases. Tex units are a measure of linear density, being the number of grammes per kilometre.

Fabrics are tested for strength, wear, thickness, air permeability, and other properties, including resistance to shrinking and fastness of dyestuffs to light and to perspiration. In strength testing, the breaking load and extension of a strip of cloth fastened between two grips is measured, tests being made in both warp and weft directions. Wear testing is done by an automatic rubbing machine which treats the specimen evenly and in all directions for a pre-set number of cycles. Thickness measurements have to be made by means of instruments exerting a very light compression so that the nap, which may be an important property of the cloth, is not unduly disturbed; for some cloths, however, heavy pressure can be used. Amongst other physical tests are those for assessing permeability to air and repellency to water.

No dyestuff can be expected to be fast to light, washing, and perspiration under all conditions of use, so the dyer must know the requirements for a yarn or cloth to enable him to select dyes with appropriate fastness properties. Most of these tests come under the two broad headings of actual and laboratory tests. Light fastness can be tested by exposure to sunlight, or to an artificial source of light, usually an enclosed carbon arc. Washing fastness can be tested by putting samples through a laundering process or by a laboratory washing process. Similarly with fastness to perspiration, actual wear tests can be made, or an artificial perspiration solution of sodium chloride may be used.

All of these tests on yarns and fabrics call for a large number of calculations to be made in the course of quality control schemes in a factory, unless tables or other devices are used to lessen the work. For this reason increasing use is being made of nomograms. A nomogram is essentially a graph in which each of the variables in a calculation is represented by a graduated scale, the value required being read from another scale. For example, in a nomogram for finding the calculated weight of a piece of cloth, a ruler is placed across the two variable scales: the piece length (say

60 yards) and the number of ounces per yard (say 15); the required piece weight is then read off the third scale (56 lb). Wira has constructed many nomograms for general use, and others for particular requirements.

Some Literature on Testing and Control

ANON., *Identification of Textile Materials*, Textile Institute, 5th edn., 1965. An authoritative book useful to all concerned. New matter in this edition includes application of infrared spectroscopy, gas chromatography, and differential thermal analysis, to fibre analysis.

ANON., *Testing and Control in the Wool Industry*, Wool Industries Research Association, 1955. Those mainly responsible for the work in each chapter are listed in the preface. Results of research work, including descriptions of instruments and testing techniques, are described in such a way that all can understand. The subjects covered are: measurement and control of humidity in testing rooms; sampling of wool fibres; fibre measurement; roving and yarn irregularity; determination of mean count and the control of quality; measurement of yarn strength; continuous strength testing of yarns; measurement of yarn twist; testing of woollen card slivers and slubbings for weight variation; testing of fabrics for strength, wear, thickness, and air permeability; testing for water repellency; nomograms; mill experiments and operational research; determination of the oil content of tops and similar material; and shrinkage testing of hosiery fabrics and garments.

BELL, J. W., *Practical Textile Chemistry*, National Trade Press, 1955. Part of the book is devoted to fibre identification and analysis, and another part to the testing of such auxiliaries as soaps and oils. The chemistry of wool is covered suitably for both teacher and student.

BOOTH, J. E., *Principles of Textile Testing*: *an introduction to physical methods of testing textile fibres, yarns, and fabrics,*

National Trade Press, 2nd edn., 1964. Useful for students of associateship examinations for the Textile Institute courses leading to degrees and diplomas in textile technology and Higher National courses in textiles. There are sections on simple statistics, sampling, moisture relations and testing, fibre dimensions and quality, yarn and fabric testing, and on various testing instruments, but not on chemical testing.

BREARLEY, A., and COX, D. R., *An Outline of Statistical Methods for Use in the Textile Industry*, Wira, 5th edn., 1961. This book has proved its value in educational establishments and in factories through five editions. Mathematics and theoretical argument are reduced to a minimum, and yet it deals adequately with such matters as the determination of the significance of differences between test results, and the statistical concepts in connection with quality control.

BROWNLEE, K. A., *Industrial Experimentation*, HMSO, 4th edn., 1949. Assumes a fair knowledge of mathematics and statistics. It deals with the design of experiments and evaluation of data, mostly in chemistry.

CLAYTON, E., *Identification of Dyes on Textile Fibres*, Society of Dyers and Colourists, 2nd edn., 1963. An authoritative practical work.

ENRICK, N. L., *Time Study Manual for the Textile Industry*, Interscience, 1960.

GARNER, W., *Textile Laboratory Manual*, National Trade Press, 1966 and 1967. Published in 6 volumes. Vol. 1: *Qualitative Methods*. Vol. 2: *Resins and Finishes*. Vol. 3: *Detergents*. Vol. 4: *Dyestuffs*. Vol. 5: *Fibres*. Vol. 6: *Additional Methods*. Essentially a practical book for all concerned with laboratory work.

GEE, N. C., *Textile Calculations*, British-Continental Trade Press, 1955. Suitable for teachers, students, and for general use.

GROVER, E. B., and HAMBY, D. S., *Handbook of Textile Testing and Quality Control*, Interscience, 1960.

LOMAX, J., *Textile Testing*, Longmans, 3rd edn., 1956. Covers identification of textile fibres, yarn and cloth dissection, burning tests, sampling, regain, yarn and cloth tests, tempera- ture and humidity control, statistical examination of results, raw wool testing, oil content, dye fastness, shrinkage tests, and water repellency. A good general book.

LUNIAK, B., *The Identification of Textile Fibres: qualitative and quantitative analysis of fibre blends*, Pitman, 1953. Translated by the author on the same lines as the 1945 German text. Part 1 includes a list of fibres, preparation of samples, and the use of the microscope. Part 2—Qualitative analysis. Part 3—Quantitative analysis. Part 4 consists of an atlas of photomicrographs.

MURPHY, T., NORRIS, K. P., and TIPPETT, L. H. C., *Statistical Methods for Textile Technologists*, Textile Institute, 1960. A practical handbook for use in processing.

O'CONNOR, T. F., *Profitable Productivity*, Emmot & Co., 1967. For work study officers and others: useful, easily under- standable material on such subjects as multiple machine assignment, redeployment of labour, and wage incentive schemes.

STRONG, J. H., *Textile Calculations Simplified*, National Trade Press, 1954. For students and technologists.

B.S. Handbook No. 11, *Methods of Test for Textiles* (see p. 89).

International Wool Secretariat Articles

The following articles in the International Wool Secretariat's series, *Wool Science Review*, are intended mainly for the textile scientist and technologist:

ONIONS, W. J., Measurement of the strength of fabrics, No. 16, p. 23, Nov. 1956.

MONFORT, F., and ANDERSON, S. L. (advised in preparation of article), Air-flow methods for measuring wool fibre dia- meter, No. 18, p. 51, Oct. 1960.

DOWNES, J. G., The determination of regain in wool, No.19, p. 20, June 1961.

ANDERSON, S. L., Neps in worsted slivers—origin, constitution, and estimation, No. 22, p. 28, March 1963.

ANDERSON, S. L., Automation of wool fibre-length measurement, No. 28, p. 22, Nov. 1965.

ZAHN, H., Chemical test methods in wool processing, No. 32, p. 1, July 1967.

ANDERSON, S. L., Abrasion and service testing of fabrics, No. 32, p. 16, July 1967.

MEDLEY, J. A., Relaxation phenomena and shrinkage testing in woven woollen cloth, No. 33, p. 19, Oct. 1967.

Wool Industries Research Association Leaflets

This Association has developed many testing devices, both for the research laboratory and for use in the industry for quality control. Some—such as the following—are in commercial production, and illustrated leaflets giving brief descriptions and names of makers, are available to bona fide inquirers. The name of each instrument is prefixed by the term Wira.

Fibre Diagram Machine. Gives a permanent record of the distribution of fibre length in a sample of tops.

Fibre Length Machine. Measures semi-automatically the length of individual fibres.

Fibre Fineness Meter. Measures the average diameter or thickness of the fibres in a sample of wool top or sliver.

Improved Rapid Regain Tester. Measures regain of fibres in a few minutes on the "drying and weighing" principle.

Rapid Oil Extraction Apparatus. Measures oil content of top and similar material in less than 15 minutes.

Roving Levelness Tester. Provides a continuous record of the thickness of worsted slivers (from tops to roving).

Cop Grader. Sorts cops of woollen yarn into weight groups, thus grading them by yarn count.

Abrasion Machine. Compares the resistance of fabrics to rubbing (up to four specimens simultaneously).

Carpet Abrasion Machine. For comparative testing like the above, but for one specimen at a time.

Carpet Thickness Gauge. Applies pressures from about 18 to 800 g/cm².

Tuft Withdrawal Tensometer. Measures the force required to withdraw a single tuft of pile from a carpet.

Dynamic Loading Machine. Simulates two of the main effects of walking on a carpet—compression, and the shearing effect at the edge of a shoe.

Autocount. Measures, records and controls automatically, variations along the length of woollen slubbing during carding.

Yarn Tension Meter. Gives steady readings of the average tension in a running yarn even if the tension is fluctuating violently.

Electrical Hygrometer. Measures relative humidity in the interior of bales or rolls of textile material.

Rapid Drying Oven. For drying and weighing tests. The oven will bring a 1 lb sample of wool or any other textile fibres from normal regain (moisture content) to dry weight at an accuracy of 0·02 g in from 4 to 6 min.

Automatic Recording Balance. For weighing and automatically recording the weight of large numbers of short lengths of woollen slubbing in a short time.

Warp Tension Meter. Measures the tension of a group of warp threads during weaving.

Heated Drum Wrap Reel. For rapid determination of count at correct condition.

The following Wira test methods leaflets can be bought from the Association:

Acid Content of Wool.
Calcium Content of Wool.
Chromium Content of Wool.
Solubility Methods for Chemical Modification of Wool (alkali solubility and urea-bisulphite solubility).
Solvent-soluble Matter in Wool.
Pentachlorophenol Content of Wool.

Unsaponifiable Matter in Oils, Fats, and Solvent Extracts from Wool.

Iodine Value of Oils and Solvent Extracts from Wool: semi-micro method.

Free Fatty Acids in Oils and Solvent Extracts from Wool.

Mineral Oil or Wax in Wool Oils and in Solvent Extracts from Wool.

Non-ionic Surface-active Agents in Oils and Solvent Extracts from Wool.

Mackey Test on Wool Oils.

Viscosity of Oils and Solvent Extracts from Wool.

The pH *Value of Water Extracts from Wool.*

Diphenylamine (Anti-Oxidant) in Wool Oils.

Total Sulphur Dioxide in Wool.

Copper, Iron, and Lead in Wool.

TEXTILE DESIGN

The textile designer must have both artistic and technical skills, and these skills will be evident in the final cloth or garment. In the retail trade colour and design are often the main selling factors, whatever the material may be; and the structural properties of the cloth—its strength, weight, dimensional stability, resistance to abrasion, wind and rain, and many other properties—depend much on the design of the weave.

Special squared paper, known as point paper, is used by the designer to indicate the order in which the warp and weft threads are to interlace in the cloth (Fig. 9). Each small square on the point paper represents the interweaving of a warp and weft thread. In order to produce the design for a woven material the designer must have a good knowledge of the type of loom on which it will be produced and its potentialities. For he has to indicate the order in which the warp threads must be drawn through the heald eyes (the "draft") and the order in which the healds must be raised and lowered (the weaving or "pegging plan"). Woven designs ranging from plain weaves and twills to elaborate floral designs can be indicated on point paper. In a complicated design the outline is first drawn in lightly, and then the squares are filled in keeping to the original conception of the design as closely as may be practicable.

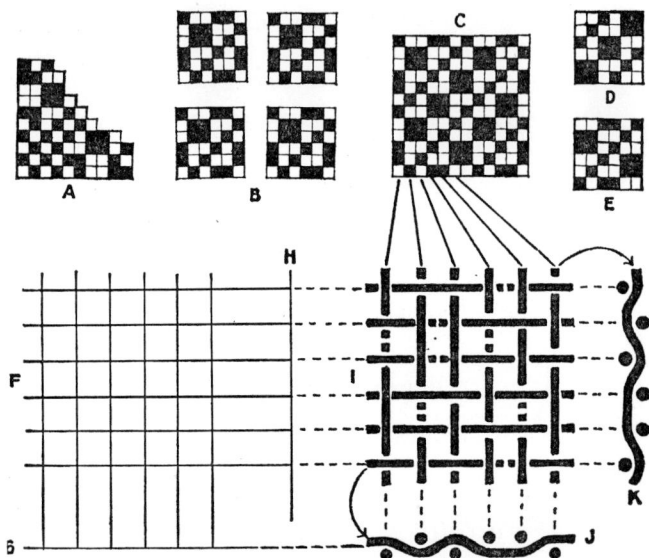

FIG. 9. From design paper to cloth. (From *Textile Design and Colour* by William Watson, Longmans.)

British Textile Designers' Guild

The Guild was formed in June 1966 following a suggestion made at the Bradford Textile Society's Design Conference in March 1966; the suggestion was that of Mr. Dennis Clive, who was then United Kingdom Director of the International Wool Secretariat. The opening meeting of the Guild was held at Bradford in October 1966.

One of the main objects of the Guild is to enable textile designers to meet and exchange views with leading designers from other fields. The Guild provides a forum also for discussions between textile designers and clothing designers and manufacturers, and a platform for speakers from the fine arts and other fields of interest to designers.

Education for Textile Designers

Information regarding courses for textile designers can be obtained from the regional advisory councils for further education listed on p. 7.

There is a School of Textile Design at the Royal College of Art, Kensington Gore, London, S.W.7 (which became a university in 1968), in which training is given in design for woven and printed textiles; the weaving department is equipped with such machinery as power- and hand-operated Dobby and Jacquard looms.

Amongst the Yorkshire universities and colleges offering full-time courses in textile design are the University of Leeds, the University of Bradford, Bradford Regional College of Art, Bradford Technical College, Huddersfield College of Technology, Leeds College of Art, Dewsbury and Batley Technical and Art College, Hull College of Art, Doncaster School of Art, Sheffield College of Art.

The Newport Monmouthshire College of Art is referred to on p. 182.

Some Literature on Textile Design

BEAUMONT, R., *Colour in Woven Design*, 1890. This excellent book still provides a source of ideas for designers.

NISBET, H., *The Grammar of Textile Design*. Benn, 1927. Useful for students.

READ, J. H., *Elementary Design and Fabric Structure*, Textile Institute, 1951. Useful for students.

ROBINSON, A. T. C., and MARKS, R., *Woven Cloth Construction*, Butterworth, 1967. A systematic study of the simpler types of woven fabrics.

STRONG, J., *Foundations of Fabric Structure*, National Trade Press, 1946. A practical book for the designer.

WATSON, W., *Advanced Textile Design*, Longmans, 3rd edn., 1947. Deals with compound and special classes of cloth.

WATSON, W., *Textile Design and Colour*, Longmans, 6th edn., 1954 (revised by Taylor, E. G., and Buchanan, J.), new impression 1956. The sub-title is "Elementary weaves and figured fabrics." In addition to the various weaves and designs, other topics are covered such as: colour theories and phenomena; application of colour; Jacquard machines.

WRIGHT, R. H., *Modern Textile Design and Production*, National Trade Press, 1949. Useful to commercial artists and art school students wishing to apply their skill in textiles.

YORKSHIRE COUNCIL FOR FURTHER EDUCATION, *The Textile Designer in Industry*, 1964. This is a report by the County Advisory Committee for Textile Industries, the contents being: the designer in industry; existing full-time courses for textile designers in the region; three categories of textile designers; existing part-time provision in Yorkshire; information from overseas; comments and conclusions. Copies of this pamphlet (No. 82, May 1964), are available from the Secretary, Yorkshire Council for Further Education, Bowling Green Terrace, Jack Lane, Leeds, 11.

introduction of the cotton warp, which cheapened worsteds and enabled the growing masses of industrial population to buy them. Alpaca and mohair also added a fillip to the trade. Finally, however, from about 1870 onwards, it was good quality worsteds for which Bradford became and has remained famous.

While Bradford is noted mainly for its large production of medium quality worsted cloths for men's suitings and ladies' dress goods, Huddersfield has a worldwide reputation for the finest of worsted fabrics; the mills in the Huddersfield area (which includes Brighouse, Holmfirth, Kirkburton, Meltham, Saddleworth, the Colne Valley, Holme Valley, and Denby Dale) use high-quality merino wools for their fine worsteds. In addition to fine worsteds, Huddersfield is renowned for fine woollens and woollens of all types. Keighley and district (including Bingley, Denholme, and Silsden) has many worsted spinning and weaving mills. In the Halifax district (including Hebden Bridge, Sowerby Bridge, Ripponden, Heptonstall, Todmorden, and Elland) and Wakefield, there is mostly worsted spinning, and also worsted weaving. In Keighley and Halifax there are also textile machinery manufacturers.

Mungo and shoddy manufacturers are mostly located in what is known as the "heavy woollen" district of Dewsbury, Batley, and Ossett, including also Mirfield, Morley, Spenborough, and Heckmondwike.

Leeds, including Horsforth and Pudsey, is the centre for the making-up trade, and there are also some firms of woollen and worsted manufacturers in the district.

WEST OF ENGLAND

During the Tudor period, cloths from the West of England were by far the most important export from this country. The trade remained important during the seventeenth century, but lost ground to the West Riding of Yorkshire in the eighteenth century. The period of the Industrial Revolution brought troublesome times, and the machine breakers caused much damage both to individual plant and to the industry as a whole. The decline in trade continued throughout the nineteenth century; but the West of England still retains its traditional reputation for woollen cloths of the highest quality that require special finishes.

There are three main centres of this old-established industry: Stroud, Trowbridge, and Witney, the latter concentrating almost entirely on blankets. There are also factories in Westbury, Cam, Frome, Ashburton, and several other towns.

Most of the cloths made are very typical of the West Country trade. Heavily milled cloth is made for billiard cloths, tennis ball cases, doeskins, and melton overcoatings. One firm in Gloucestershire produces some unusual specialities such as cloths for the Papal Court, and a fabric used as a background for displaying the royal jewels. The traditional Guards uniform cloth is also made in this area.

In the Wiltshire area there are several manufacturers of fancy woollens for both the men's and ladies' trade, and also superfine worsteds; and there is a manufacturer of fancy woollens at Chipping Norton in Oxfordshire.

At Wellington in Somerset there is a large worsted and woollen firm which is organized vertically for worsted as well as woollen, this being somewhat unusual; they carry out all the worsted stages of processing from scouring and combing on to finishing.

Saxony tweeds are made largely in the West of England; the fabric is smooth and soft in handle and may have a clear or dress face finish.

WALES

The Welsh woollen industry has been decreasing in size during the last 50 years or so. Before the First World War there were about 250 mills in Wales; in 1953 there were about 60; now (1967) there are about 25. During the depression of the 1920's and the slump of the following decade, the industry was badly hit; the replacement of machinery was an economic impossibility for many firms—most of which were, and still are, small family concerns in the real meaning of the word, some being run by a family of three or four. Let it be understood, however, that the industry is not dying: far from it.

The Rural Industries Bureau (see p. 96) has done, and is doing, a great deal to bring about the renaissance of a fine old traditional industry which is a potential asset to the national economy. The Wool, Jute, and Flax Industry Training Board (see p. 66) is co-operating in this effort in many ways. For example, a textile designer on the staff of the RIB has attended an instructor's course organized by the Training Board, and this designer is working within the companies in the industry. In 1966–7 the Training Board, in association with the RIB, held a series of meetings to promote a Welsh Woollen Group Training Scheme, the benefit of which is being appreciated by the Welsh manufacturers. A course for instructors organized and run by the Training Board in 1967 was well supported by the industry.

There are (1967) no technical colleges in Wales with textile departments; students wishing to undertake advanced training go, as a rule, to the Scottish Woollen Technical College at Galashiels, or to one of the colleges in the West Riding of Yorkshire. Firms in Wales are encouraged to take advantage of the grant and levy procedure of the Training Board to enable them to send apprentices and others to these colleges. There was once a Welsh Woollen Manufacturers' Association, and the revival of such an organization would undoubtedly be of benefit in co-ordinating the efforts of the industry in the promotion of their products, for which there would be a considerable demand in suitable marketing conditions.

The present industry is spread throughout the length and breadth of the country, but there is still a small concentration in and around Llandyssul and Haverfordwest, where once there was a large number of small mills. There is also a sprinkling of firms in the north in Caernarvonshire. Most of the firms are very small, employing less than 30 people; only one, a subsidiary of a Lancashire firm, in Pembroke, employs more than 100 people. One mill, near Llanwrtyd Wells in Breconshire, which is sponsored by the British Legion, provides employment for disabled people, mostly ex-service men.

The products of the Welsh industry are varied. The tweeds are hard wearing and are made in both heavy and light weight. The traditional type of blanket is the cartheni (plural carthenau), woven in bright and pastel shades, which may be regarded as a type of quilt. Another characteristic product is the honeycomb quilt. Furnishing materials, including tapestries, are made for the London market in modern styles and patterns. Other products include ties, scarves, socks, flannel shirts (particularly for mine and steel workers), overcoatings, hand knitting yarns, and yarns for hand weaving. Local Welsh wool is used, but the bulk of the raw material today is of the New Zealand crossbred type.

Although it has been stated above that there is (1967) no technical college in Wales with a textile department, it should be noted that the Newport Monmouthshire College of Art is building up a useful Textile Department which already has firm links with the industry. Besides offering full-time courses leading to Advanced City and Guilds of London Institute Certificates and the Full Technological Certificate, the Textiles Department works in close co-operation with the Painting and Sculpture Departments and the School of Graphic Design.

SCOTLAND

Scottish woollens are being produced in many parts of the country from Shetland in the north to Galloway in the south, and from the Outer Hebrides and Oban to many districts on the east coast. The biggest concentration, however, is in the Border country where about half of the cloth is made. The principal centre of the Borders is Galashiels, where there are over 20 mills, other places engaged in the industry being Selkirk, Hawick, Langholm, Peebles, Innerleithen, Walkerburn, Stow, Biggar, Earlston, and Jedburgh. There are also woollen manufacturing areas around Glasgow, the Clyde Valley, and Ayrshire; in the Hillfoots country around Alva, Tillicoultry, and Alloa; and in the north stretching from Aberdeen through Keith and Elgin to Inverness and Brora. The production of Harris Tweed is the main occupation of the population of Lewis and Harris, Stornoway (in Lewis) being the centre of the industry. Knitwear is the main product of Shetland, but light-weight tweed is also woven on hand looms.

The Scottish woollen industry as a whole is primarily occupied with the production of tweed, mostly Cheviots and Saxonies. A typically Scottish cloth is exemplified by thornproof suiting made from Cheviot quality wool, which may be a blend of New Zealand crossbred and home-grown Cheviot wool. Its hard-wearing qualities are conferred by the hard-twisted twofold yarn, which give the cloth a crisp handle, and by the plain weave. Cheviot overcoating is of looser construction, and may be woven from a combination of woollen and worsted yarns. Another typical Scottish tweed is a saxony suiting in a well-defined check design, such as Glen Urquhart check, made from high quality Merino wool.

In addition to woollens, the Scottish industry produces such worsted cloths as tropical suitings, ladies' dress cloths, gabardines, and many other cloths including rugs, scarves, stoles, and tie material. There are over 300 authentic designs of tartan, which may be all worsted or have, for example, a twofold worsted warp and a single woollen weft, the overall appearance being of worsted. Tartans are now finding new outlets as furnishings; and many other types of furnishing fabric are produced by the Scottish industry.

Although home-grown wool and wools from Australia, New Zealand, and South Africa provide the bulk of the raw material for the industry, many other fibres are used. Some of these are camel hair from the Middle East; cashmere from China, Outer Mongolia, and Tibet; mohair from South Africa; alpaca from Peru; angora from France and Turkey; and even reindeer hair from Lapland.

Cashmere, particularly for knitwear, is becoming increasingly popular. Although the major output is of sweaters, cardigans, and twin sets, an increasing interest is being taken in the use of cashmere for men's sports jackets, and overcoats for both men and women. The marketing interests of cashmere as a finished product are watched and safeguarded by the Scottish Cashmere Association, a consortium of spinners and knitters, which both promotes the product at home and abroad, and seeks to prevent infringement of the word "cashmere".

The Scottish knitwear industry is very widespread, but the production of high quality knitted outerwear is centred mostly in Hawick and the surrounding area. The products of this area are exported to some ninety markets overseas, the value of this export being about £7 m., or approximately half the total production. The Hawick Knitwear Manufacturers' Association caters for the manufacturers in Hawick. Other organizations are the Scottish Hosiery and Knitwear Manufacturers' Association and the Scottish Hosiery Manufacturers' Federation.

Exports of Scottish tweeds (excluding orb-marked Harris Tweed) for 1966 amounted to nearly £7 m.—about 45 per cent of total production.

The National Association of Scottish Woollen Manufacturers

The Association, which is a member of the Wool Textile Delegation, represents the majority of the firms in the Scottish woollen industry. A useful guide to its membership and to the industry in general is given by the Association's handbook, *The Scottish Woollen Industry*. Members are listed by categories—spinner manufacturers; manufacturers; sale yarn spinners; and dyers and finishers; they are also listed alphabetically with details of their products. There is a classified list in tabular form showing the products of each member firm and the names of all member firms producing any specific item, and a geographical guide to the mills in the industry.

Scottish Woollen Publicity Council

This is a partnership formed by representatives of the Scottish woollen industry and the International Wool Secretariat. The Council's certification trade mark, embodying a St. Andrew's Cross and a thistle, and the words "Fine Woollens Woven in Scotland" (Fig. 10), is an assurance that the cloth is made of pure

FIG. 10. Scottish Woollens—certification trade mark. (By permission of the International Wool Secretariat.)

new wool and that it has been designed and woven in Scotland. The cross and thistle symbol can be used only by firms that are members of the Council; it is used alone for cloth and, with a variation in the wording, for yarn. It is combined with the Woolmark (see p. 100) for garments.

Scottish Woollen Designers' Group

The group was formed in 1959 under the auspices of the National Association of Scottish Woollen Manufacturers. It provides a forum for exchange of ideas and experience, and designers obtain much benefit from the regular meetings, discussions, conferences, and visits. Some examples of visits made by the group are: to a newly commissioned Ben Line ship; the Gallery of Modern Art in Edinburgh; and to clothing manufacturing firms.

Further Information

Appropriate inquiries regarding the Scottish woollen industry should be addressed to:

> The National Association of Scottish Woollen Manufacturers,
> 27 Charlotte Square,
> Edinburgh, 2.

Harris Tweed

After many years of litigation Lord Hunter gave judgement in 1964 in the Court of Session in Edinburgh, ruling that a cloth to be called Harris Tweed must at least conform to the Harris Tweed Association's 1935 definition: it must be made from pure virgin Scottish wool, dyed, spun, and finished in the Outer Hebrides, and hand woven at the homes of the islanders. True Harris Tweed is stamped every three yards on the reverse side of the cloth with the well-known orb and Maltese cross (Fig. 11) after it has been examined and approved by the inspectors of The Harris Tweed Association Ltd.

Cloth has been spun and woven from local wool on hand looms in Harris and Lewis for many hundreds of years. The fascinating story of the growth of this craft into a flourishing export industry can be read in the Scott Report of 1913, produced by Professor Scott of St. Andrew's University. Some of the early history and the details of the above litigation are given in *"Harris Tweed" Case (Trade Description, Trade Libel) Reports of Patent, Design and Trade Mark Cases, No. 16, 1964,* edited by T. A. Blanco White, Barrister-at-law, obtainable from Patent Office, 25 Southampton Buildings, Chancery Lane, London, W.C.2. This document also gives a good account of the traditional methods of making the cloth.

Today, natural dyes are still used by a few weavers i   H
who do all the processes by hand and market their
With this exception only chemical dyes are now used in
plants, the two main reasons being: (a) exact matching
for repeat orders would be impossible, (b) the Islands w
be stripped of vegetation if natural dyes were used to
demands of today. Hand carding and spinning are now
obsolete, and the "waulking" of the cloth (fulling by
kneading it) by women, described by James Boswell in *Th*
of a Tour to the Hebrides, is no longer done.

There are now (1967) six spinning and finishing mills in St
way and one at Shawbost on the west side of Lewis, and a carding

Fig. 11. Harris Tweed—the orb and Maltese cross. (By permission
of the Harris Tweed Association Ltd.)

mill in Tarbert, Harris. A small spinning mill in North Uist
is expected to be reopened in the near future. The standard loom
used today is the Hattersley Domestic Loom, which is operated
by hand and foot.

Harris Tweed is exported to about thirty countries and is an
important dollar earner, the United States being the largest single
export customer, taking between 20–25 per cent of the total output. Production of stamped cloth is rising steadily; in 1961 the
total yardage was about 5 million, and in 1966 over $7\frac{1}{2}$ million,
67 per cent of which was exported.

The Harris Tweed Association Ltd., whose headquarters are at
92 Academy Street, Inverness, was formed in 1909, and the
certification mark was finally approved in 1911. The Association
is not a trading company, and its members are private individuals

who have no financial stake in the industry: no manufacturing firms, producers, or weavers are members. The Association holds the certification mark in trust for the Islanders and is charged with the duty of furthering the interests of Harris Tweed and policing and protecting the industry as a whole.

Highland Home Industries

More than 100 years ago various organizations were formed to preserve local and traditional industries in the Highlands and Islands, to maintain and improve the standard of work, and to market the goods produced. Most of the local and unrelated effort were gradually combined to form the Highland Home Industries Ltd., a non-profit-making organization which established a selling centre at 94 George Street, Edinburgh, 2. Sales from branches, and by means of mail order business throughout the British Isles and overseas, have risen from £3000 in 1914 and £60,000 in 1954 to £125,000 in 1966.

This organization buys from craftsmen working in their own homes such goods as tweeds, rugs, ties, and knitwear of many kinds; purchases are also made from small Scottish firms seeking to expand their markets.

The Highland Home Industries employ two organizers who advise on such matters as design, so as to ensure that the goods produced will be readily marketable. In addition, there is a weaving and training centre at Morar.

NORTHERN IRELAND

The wool textile industry in Northern Ireland is small but very versatile, and during the period immediately following the Second World War there was a tendency for new firms to be established. Hand-woven tweeds of distinctive design have for long been exported to countries all over the world; and they still are, some from quite small mills operating hand looms in addition to modern weaving machines. But the industry today is essentially modern in its methods, and above all keenly export-minded.

The industry is located largely in Co. Antrim, but there are factories also in the counties of Armagh, Down, Fermanagh, and Tyrone. There is both worsted and woollen spinning, white and coloured yarns being spun in all-wool and blends of wool and man-made fibres, and wool and linen, for weaving, hand knitting, hosiery, and carpets. Amongst the wide diversity of men's and ladies' tweeds being produced are Donegal, Irish, Bannockburn, Cheviot, Saxonies, thornproofs, and homespuns. Other types of cloth woven in Northern Ireland are overcoatings, friezes, hopsacks, tie cloths, cap cloths, and blankets. Carpets and rugs are also manufactured, some of the wool being dyed (loose wool, slubbing and yarn) in Northern Ireland.

Northern Ireland Wool Users' Association

83 High Street, Belfast, 1.

This employers' organization consists of the major woollen and worsted manufacturers and spinners in Northern Ireland. They meet regularly to exchange ideas and discuss trade and other business of interest. The Association, which is a representative member of the Wool Textile Delegation, negotiates with the local trade unions in Northern Ireland. For their size, the firms in this group are the largest exporters of cloth and yarn in the British Isles. The output of cloth is in the region of 6–7 million yards per year; and with the high standard of design and marketing this is likely to increase.

SOME BOOKS OF REFERENCE ON THE INDUSTRY

The latest edition of these books can be ascertained from *Whitaker's Cumulative Book List:*

British and Commonwealth Textile Industry, John Worrall Ltd., Oldham.
Continental WOOLINDEX, John Worrall Ltd., Oldham.

Skinner's Wool Trade Directory of the World. Thomas Skinner & Co., Bradford.

Textile Machinery Index, John Worrall Ltd., Oldham.

Wool Year Book, Textile Mercury, Salford.

Yorkshire Textile Industry, John Worrall Ltd., Oldham.

APPENDIX I

A Short Reading List on the History of Sheep and their Wool

British Wool Manual, Harlequin Press, 2nd edn., 1968. The first section, by Lemon, H., deals briefly with the origin and development of domestic breeds, including Merino and Crossbreds.

COX, E. W., *The Evolution of the Australian Merino*, Angus & Robertson, Sydney, 1936. The early introduction of the breed from various countries is described, and also the evolution of most of the studs.

LUCCOCK, J. *The Nature and Properties of Wool*, 1805. This book, by a "Wool-stapler", was the standard book of its period.

PONTING, K. G., *The Wool Trade Past and Present*, Columbine Press, 1961. After an historical introduction in the first two chapters, most of the book is concerned with the Merino, first in Spain and Germany, then in Australia.

RYDER, M. L., The history of sheep breeds in Britain, *Agric. History Rev. 12* (1) 1–12, (2) 65–82 (1964). A synthesis of historical and biological evidence giving a modern view of breed origins.

TROW-SMITH, R., *English Husbandry: from the earliest times to the present day*, Faber & Faber, 1951. Chapter 9 examines the modification of sheep breeds to modern types.

TROW-SMITH, R., *A History of British Livestock Husbandry to 1700*, Routledge & Kegan Paul, 1957. Chapter 4 is on medieval sheep husbandry.

TROW-SMITH, R., *A History of British Livestock Husbandry 1700–1900*, Routledge & Kegan Paul, 1959. A sequel to his earlier book above.

YOUATT, W., *Sheep, their Breeds, Management, and Diseases*, London, 1837. Both wild sheep and British domestic breeds are described.

A Short Reading List on Sheep and Wool Today

APPLEYARD, H. M., *Guide to the Identification of Animal Fibres*, Wool Industries Research Association, Leeds, 1960. The major part of the book consists of an alphabetical table of animal fibres, descriptions of them and photomicrographs.

Annual Review of the Australian Wool Clip, Dennys Lascelles Ltd., 26–32 Moorabool Street, Geelong, Victoria, Australia. Exports of wool are analysed. Comments are made on such subjects as the effects of private selling on auction prices, and on the preparation of the clip.

BERGEN, W. (Ed.), *Wool Handbook*, Vol. 1, 3rd edn., Wiley, New York, 1963. Although published in the United States, this book can be regarded as a major standard work of reference in Britain on sheep breeds and the structure and properties of wool and hair fibres.

British Wool Manual, Harlequin Press, 2nd edn., 1968. See pp. 131 and 191.

BRITISH WOOL MARKETING BOARD (in co-operation with the International Wool Secretariat), *British Sheep Breeds: their wool and its uses*, 1967. A useful book for anybody interested in sheep and wool.

HAIGH, H., and NEWTON, B. A., *The Wools of Britain*, Pitman, 1952. Descriptions and textile uses of British wools.

HIND, J. R., *Woollen and Worsted Raw Materials*, Ernest Benn, 2nd edn., 1948. The various wools, hairs, and other textile raw materials are described.

NATIONAL SHEEP BREEDERS ASSOCIATION, *British Sheep*, 1968. This is a second edition of *British Pure-Bred Sheep*, which was published in 1946. Each breed is illustrated and briefly described.

ONIONS, W. J., *Wool: an introduction to its properties, varieties, production, and uses*, Ernest Benn, 1962. See p. 129.

RYDER, M. L., and STEPHENSON, S. K., *Wool Growth*, Academic Press, 1967. Recent research on wool growth and fleece variation, from the sheep, its domestication and the development of breeds, to wool textile processes.

WILDMAN, A. B., *The Microscopy of Animal Textile Fibres*, Wool Industries Research Association, Leeds, 1954. The technique of sampling and preparing fibres for microscopy, the classification of fibre features, quantitative analysis of fibre mixtures, and the diagnostic uses of photomicrography (by Appleyard, H. M.). The fibres of sheep and other animals are discussed and their distinctive features are lavishly illustrated by photomicrographs.

APPENDIX 3

A Short Reading List on Wool Textile History

ANON., Perkin Centenary, London, *100 Years of Synthetic Dyestuffs*, Pergamon Press, 1958. Contains: Foreword by Sir Robert Robinson; "The life and works of Perkin" by John Read; "The development of the dyestuffs industry" by Clifford Paine; "The tinctorial arts of today" by John Gwynant Evans; "The development of organic chemistry since Perkin's discovery" by Sir Alexander Todd.

BOWDEN, P. J., *The Wool Trade in Tudor and Stuart England*, Macmillan, 1962. Amongst the many topics dealt with authoritatively are: sheep and types of wool and their uses for different fabrics; broadcloth and medley cloth in the West of England; the new draperies; cloths in Yorkshire; Alderman Cockayne's scheme for dyeing and dressing cloth in Britain.

BURNLEY, J., *The History of Wool and Woolcombing*, London, 1889. Contains much general information on textile processing in addition to combing, and includes accounts of Cartwright's inventions in combing and weaving in the inventor's own words.

BURROWS, H., *A History of the Rag Trade*, Maclaren & Sons, 1956. Origin of the shoddy and mungo trade in the early nineteenth century, of the carbonizing of rags to remove cotton in the early 1850's, and the development of the trade.

CLARK, C. O., Ancient and modern in milling and scouring, *J. Soc. Dyers and Colourists*, March 1950. Authentic information not readily found elsewhere, such as descriptions of different types of fulling stocks for scouring and milling.

CRUMP, W. B. (Ed.), *The Leeds Woollen Industry 1780–1820*, the Thoresby Society, Leeds, 1931. Information on Benjamin Gott, the merchant-manufacturer, scribbling mills and their machinery, fulling mills, cropping shops, types of cloth. The book also includes the Diary of Joseph Rogerson, Scribbling Miller, of Bramley, 1808–14, and the Bean Ing Mill Notebook. The latter gives details of mill practice of the period.

CRUMP, W. B., and GHORBAL, G., *History of the Huddersfield Woollen Industry*, Tolson Memorial Museum, Huddersfield, 1935. Provides a good picture of the West Riding wool textile industry during the fourteenth to eighteenth centuries inclusive.

DANIELS, G. W., *The Early English Cotton Industry*, Longmans (publications of the University of Manchester), 1920. A very readable book covering the development and organization of the industry and the introduction of machinery, much of which was first used for cotton and later adapted for wool.

HEATON, H., *The Yorkshire Woollen and Worsted Industries*, Oxford University Press, 2nd edn., 1965. This is Vol. X of Oxford Historical and Literary Studies, a scholarly account of the growth of the industry from earliest times up to and including the eighteenth century. Originally published in 1920.

JAMES, J., *History of the Worsted Manufacture in England*, London, 1857. Provides an immense amount of information on general wool textile history, processing, types of cloth, mechanical inventions, and other matters. (Reprinted by Frank Cass, 1968.)

JENKINS, J. G., *The Esgair Moel Woollen Mill*, The National Museum of Wales, 1965. This eighteenth-century mill, the building and machinery, was moved from near Llanwrtyd to the Welsh Folk Museum at Cardiff. The processes described are loose wool dyeing, willeying, carding, spinning (hand mule), twisting, fulling, and finishing.

JENKINS, J. G., *The Woollen Industry in Montgomeryshire*, the Montgomery Collections, Vol. LVIII, Pt. 1, 1963. Early history, processing, marketing.

Journal of the Society of Dyers and Colourists, The Jubilee Issue (1934). Articles of historical interest: BREWIN, A. H., History of the Worshipful Company of Dyers, London; EDWARDS, W. A., and HARDCASTLE, G. F., Hosiery dyeing and finishing 1884–1934; GREEN, A. C., Landmarks in the evolution of the dyestuff industry during the past half-century; HUEBNER, J., Early history of dyeing; ISLES, E., Slubbing and wool yarn dyeing; STANSFIELD, W. S., Half a century in the dyeing and finishing of worsted, woollen, and union piece goods.

LEMON, H., Some aspects of the Early History of Spinning, *J. Textile Inst.*, 1951, P. 479. Information on carding and combing as well as spinning.

LIPSON, E., *The History of the Woollen and Worsted Industries*, Frank Cass, 1965 (first published by A. & C. Black in 1921). Gives a good general background. The chapter headings are: Origin and growth; Organisation; State control; Processes and inventions; Introduction of machinery; Geographical distribution.

MARTINDALE, J. G., Carding, evolution, and early development, *J. Textile Inst.*, 1949, P. 65. An authoritative account by one whose activities have embraced modern industry, research and education.

MENDENHALL, T. C., *The Shrewsbury Drapers and the Welsh Woollen Trade in the XVI and XVII Centuries*, Oxford University Press, 1953. An account of the Welsh trade in comparison with those of Yorkshire and the West of England.

MORRIS, G. W., and WOOD, L. S., *The Golden Fleece*, Clarendon Press, Oxford, 1922. Good account of earliest days of industry, medieval gilds, domestic system, industrial revolution.

NATIONAL ASSOCIATION OF SCOTTISH WOOLLEN MANUFACTURERS, *Scottish Woollens*. Amongst the many interesting papers in this series are: *Tartans*, No. 5, Feb. 1933 and No. 8, May 1934. *Our Scottish District Checks*, No. 6, July 1933 and No. 7, Dec. 1933. *Shetland Wool*, No. 12, July 1935.

A Word on the History of the Scottish Woollen Trade, No. 13, Oct. 1935. *Birth-place of Harris Tweeds*, No. 18, Nov. 1937. *What is Tweed?*, No. 31, Feb. 1944. *Cheviot Cloth*, No. 32, June 1944. *The Paisley Shawl*, No. 39, June 1949.

PEEL, F., *The Risings of the Luddites*, 1888. The author collected his material from people in the Heckmondwike (Yorkshire) district who were old enough to know something of the subject from personal experience.

PLUMMER, A., *The Whitney Blanket Industry*, Routledge, 1934. Information on the Company of Blanket Weavers and the organization of the industry.

PONTING, K. G., *A History of the West of England Cloth Industry*, Macdonald, 1957. A valuable aspect of this book is that the author, as a member of an old-established family firm in the West Country, can relate the practice of the present with that of the past (upon which he is very knowledgeable).

PONTING, K. G., *The Wool Trade Past and Present*, Columbine Press, 1961. The information on cloth and its manufacture, both past and present, is given by a man who has a deep understanding of the subject (see above).

POWER, E., *Medieval People*, Penguin, 1937 (first published 1924). Chapter 5 is on Thomas Betson, a merchant of the Staple in the fifteenth century. Chapter 6 is on Thomas Paycocke of Coggleshall, an Essex clothier in the days of Henry VII. Both provide delightful as well as rewarding reading.

POWER, E., *The Wool Trade in English Medieval History*, Oxford University Press, 1941. This book, comprising the Ford Lectures of 1939, is a little gem of historical literature, by a sound authority on the subject.

RAMSAY, G. D., *The Wiltshire Woollen Industry in the 16th and 17th Centuries*, Frank Cass, 2nd edn., 1965 (first published by Oxford University Press, 1943). Scholarly work based mainly on Public Record Office and similar documents. A valuable addition in the second edition is the Report of the Clothing Committee of the Privy Council, of 1622.

SIGSWORTH, E. M., *Black Dyke Mills—A History*, Liverpool University Press, 1958. The development of the worsted industry up to and including the nineteenth century. This book covers much more than the title implies, and is particularly valuable on the introduction of machine combing.

TREVELYAN, G. M., *English Social History*, Longmans, 1944. (*Illustrated English Social History*, Longmans, 4 vols, 1949–52; and Penguin, 4 vols, 1964.) Much of English social history, so well recorded in this book, was for many centuries closely related to wool growing, processing and trading.

VICKERMAN, C., *Woollen Spinning*, Macmillan, 1894. Particularly interesting, and entertaining, on the introduction of the principle of condensing (which Vickerman abhorred), which shortened the processing of woollen yarn. In one passage he describes the condensed woollen slubbing as "a pretence, a cheat, a swindle, a fraud, palmed off as a woollen thread".

WATSON, J., *The Theory and Practice of the Art of Weaving*, Glasgow, 1888. Covers weaving from ancient times to the author's day.

APPENDIX 4

Glossary of Wool Textile Terms

Abb. Skirtings of coarse wool kept separate in shearing.

Acid dyes. Dyes used mainly for wool, capable of giving a wide range of level shades.

Ageing. Practice of allowing material to rest between one stage of processing and the next.

Alpaca. Hair of the alpaca, a type of llama inhabiting mountainous districts of South America.

Angola. Yarn and cloth made from a mixture of wool and cotton.

Angora. Hair of the Angora rabbit.

Anthrax. "Woolsorters' Disease": infection is liable to come particularly from mohair, camel hair, alpaca, and cashmere. Precautions taken on import and in mills now render this disease rare.

Astrakhan. Wool from skin of young lambs with curly fleece, or curled pile fabric made in imitation of this.

Axminster. Carpet in which tufts of pile are inserted into the foundation fabric in rows weft way.

Backwashing. A worsted process: the washing of wool between carding and combing.

Baize. Felted woollen cloth with nap on both sides.

Bale. Woolpack, the weight of which depends on the country of origin.

Barathea. Cloth, usually worsted, woven in twilled hopsack, and having a pebbled appearance.

Beaming. Process of winding warp from warping beam to weaver's beam which fits to the back of the loom.

Beating-up. Action of reed in beating weft into the fell of the cloth during weaving.

Beaver. A heavy woollen cloth of firm texture which is milled, raised and given a nap finish in imitation of beaver skin.

Bedford cord. Cloth with a cord or rib effect in the warp direction.

Bellies. Coarse wool from the under side of the sheep.

Berlins. Term used in the shoddy trade to describe fine quality knitted goods.

Birdseye. Cloth with a small spot effect uniformly distributed.

Bleaching. Process for improving the whiteness of textile material.

Blending. Mixing of different types and colours of wool and other fibres before woollen carding.

Block printing. Printing of cloth by hand with wooden blocks.

Blowing. A finishing process in which steam is blown through the cloth.

Botany. Tops, yarn, and cloth made from Merino wool.

Bouclé. Cloth made from fancy yarns producing knots, loops, or curls on the surface.

Box cloth. A heavily milled woollen cloth.

Bradford system. Method of drawing and spinning worsted yarn from oil-combed tops.

Broadcloth. A stout woollen cloth made from fine quality yarns, with twill weave, and heavily milled.

Broadloom carpet. Seamless carpeting 6 ft or more in width.

Brussels. Plain or figured carpet similar to Wilton but with a loop pile.

Buckskin. Fine woollen cloth with milled and raised finish.

Bulked yarns. Yarns given some treatment to increase their bulk.

Bunting. Worsted cloth of plain weave suitable for flags.

Burling. Removal of vegetable matter and rectification of certain other faults in cloth.

Burry wool. Wool still retaining seeds and other vegetable matter originally picked up by the fleece.

Cabled yarn. Two or more plied yarns twisted together.

Camlet. Fine, thin, plain-weave cloth made from lustre yarns. (Originally made from camel hair and silk.)

Cap spinning. Method of spinning fine worsted yarns.

Carbonizing. Removal of vegetable and other cellulosic matter (such as cotton) from wool material by steeping in dilute sulphuric acid and subsequent heating.

Carding. Opening out and blending an entangled mass of fibres: used in both worsted and woollen processes.

Cashmere. Hair of Cashmere (or Kashmir) goat, remarkable for its softness.

Cavalry twill. A firm cloth with a steep double twill.

Cheese. A package of yarn in cylindrical form.

Chlorination. Treatment of wool with chlorine to confer shrink resistance and other properties.

Classing. See *Wool classing.*

Colonial wools. Wools from Australia, New Zealand, and South Africa.

Combing. Worsted process for combing the long fibres parallel and removing the short fibres before drawing and spinning.

Comeback. Wool from sheep that have been produced by crossing Merinos with fine crossbred sheep.

Condenser. That part of a woollen card (or carding machine) in which a fine film of wool is divided into strips and rubbed into slubbings for spinning.

Condition. Term used in connection with the moisture content of wool material. See also *Standard condition.*

Cone. A package of yarn in conical form.

Cop. A package of yarn conical at each end such as is spun on a mule.

Cotty Wool. Matted, felted wool in the fleece.

Count. System for giving an indication of the linear density of a yarn.

Course. Row of loops across a knitted fabric.

Crabbing. Worsted finishing process for setting the cloth so that it will not wrinkle during the subsequent wet processing; the cloth is treated with steam or boiling water while on a perforated roller.

Creel. A frame for holding bobbins or other packages.

Crimp. Natural waviness of wool fibre, or the form of the yarn as it lies in the woven cloth.

Cropping. Shearing the nap on the surface of cloth.

Crutchings. Wool of little value set aside during shearing.

Curled Yarn. Yarn producing on the surface of the cloth a curled affect.

Cut. Length of warp required to weave a piece of cloth.

Cuttling. Folding a cloth loosely between processes.

Daggings. Alternative term for crutchings.

Dead Wool. Wool removed from sheep that has died from natural causes.

Decatizing. Process in which steam or hot water is passed through cloth to enhance its lustre.

Degreasing. Removal of natural grease from wool by means of a solvent

Delaine. Light worsted cloth of plain weave, usually printed.

Dent. The wire or space between wires in a loom reed.

Devil. Term sometimes used for a kind of willey (q.v.).

Discharge printing. Method in which a cloth is dyed in a plain colour and then printed with a substance that removes the dye, thus producing a pattern.

Doeskin. Fine woollen cloth with smooth surface.

Doffing. Removal of filled bobbins from spinning or other machines.

Donegal. Characteristic Irish tweed of plain weave with speckled effect.

Double cloth. One in which two cloths, each with its own warp and weft, are woven together.

Doubling. The combination of slubbings or slivers in worsted drawing to promote evenness.

Drafting. Attenuation of slubbings, slivers or rovings in drawing or spinning. The term draft is also used for the arrangement of the warp threads in the loom.

Drawing. Series of worsted processes for drawing out the combed top before spinning.

Drawing-in. Drawing the warp threads through the heald eyes and reed of a loom preparatory to weaving.

Dry combing. Combing without added oil, usually for Continental system of worsted spinning.

Duffel. Thick woollen cloth napped on both sides (also known as *flushing*).

Dumping. Compressing bale of wool to reduce cargo volume.

Durable press (*pressing*). Finishing treatment for imparting to cloth or garments creases, pleats, or flat surface, as desired.

Ends. Individual threads of warp.

Ends down. Broken warp threads. Used similarly of slubbing, sliver, roving, and yarn.

Extract. Wool extracted from a cotton and wool mixture by carbonizing.

Face cloth. A cloth in which the warp threads predominate on one side.

Fell. The edge of the cloth during weaving formed by the last weft thread to be inserted and beaten up.

Fellmongering. Removing the wool from skins of slaughtered sheep.

Felt. Cloth in which the fibres are densely matted, there being no warp and weft structure. Cloth that is woven and then heavily felted is usually termed woven felt.

Felting. The (usually unwanted) matting together of fibres (cf. *Milling*).

Fents. Short, sometimes damaged, lengths of cloth, cut from a whole piece.

Fettling. The clearing of fibres and rubbish from between the teeth of the clothing on a carding machine.

Fingering yarn. Plied worsted yarn intended for hand knitting.

Flannel. Woollen or worsted, originally all wool, plain or twill weave cloth, usually slightly milled and raised. (Flannelette is a cotton cloth.)

Flock. Very short lengths of fibre obtained from cropping cloth and from similar processes.

Flock print. Pattern produced on cloth by printing an adhesive on the surface and applying flock by blowing or other means.

Fluorescent brightening agent. Substance applied to material for increasing the amount of visible light reflected, thus enhancing its brightness.

Flushing. See *Duffel.*

Flyer spinning. Method of worsted spinning generally for coarser yarn than that spun on cap frames.

Folded Yarn. Yarn consisting of two or more single threads.

French comb. The Heilmann comb, used for short wools.

French drawing (Continental drawing). Method of worsted drawing in which no twist is inserted until the final stage.

Frieze. Heavy woollen cloth with a rough nap.

Fulling. Now normally termed *Milling* (q.v.).

Gabardine. Closely woven cloth with twill line at a steep angle, used mostly for raincoats.

Garnett machine. Used in rag pulling.

Gilling. Early stage of worsted drawing.

Grey Piece ("piece in the grey"). Piece of cloth straight from the loom.

Hair. Fibre from animal other than sheep.

Handle. The "feel" of cloth.

Hank. Length of reeled yarn.

Harris Tweed. Genuine Harris Tweed must be 100 per cent Scottish wool and it must be spun, dyed, woven, and finished on the islands of the Outer Hebrides.

Healds (heddles). Cords, wires, or steel strips with eye through which warp threads pass in the loom so that they may be raised and lowered according to the requirements of the pattern.

Heilmann comb. Used for combing short wools.

Hogg (hog, hoggett, teg) wool. First wool from a sheep not shorn as a lamb.

Hopsack. Plain weave with two or more ends and picks weaving as one.

Hosiery. This term now covers all types of knitted fabrics.

In the grease. Wool in its natural state.

Jacquard. Loom mechanism for weaving figured designs.

Jersey cloth (fabric). Now applied generally to knitted piece-goods.

Kemp. Coarse fibres shed into the fleece periodically; after dyeing they appear lighter than normal fibres.

Keratin. Substance forming the wool fibre, composed of carbon, oxygen, nitrogen, hydrogen, and sulphur.

Kersey. Woollen cloth made from crossbred wool, milled and finished with a short nap.

Knop yarn. Fancy yarn with lumps at intervals along its length.

Lamb's wool. Wool shorn from lambs up to about 8 months old.

Laps. Soft waste from the worsted drawing process.

Linsey–Wolsey. Coarse cloth with linen warp and worsted weft.

List. See *Selvedge.*

Llama. Hair of the llama inhabiting mountainous districts of South America.

Locks. Short wool of little value, often stained.

Lofty. Term for springy wool with full handle.

London shrinking. Finishing process in which the cloth is damped and then allowed to dry in a relaxed state; the object is to avoid subsequent shrinkage after making-up.

Looming. Alternative term for *Drawing-in* (q.v.).

Matchings. The different sorts of wool into which the fleece is divided in sorting.

Medulla. Central cellular air space in an animal fibre.

Melange printing (*vigoureux printing*). Method of printing in which slubbing is printed in bands along its length; subsequent combing effects a blending of the dyed and undyed fibres.

Melton. A heavy cloth, either all wool or cotton warp and woollen weft, finished by heavy milling and cropping.

Mending. Removal of faults in a cloth by inserting new lengths of yarn to replace missing or faulty lengths.

Merino. Wool from pure-bred Merino sheep.

Milling. Wet finishing process designed to consolidate the fibres and produce a surface effect on cloth obscuring the weave to any extent required.

Mohair. Hair of the Angora goat, produced mainly in Turkey, South Africa, and the United States.

Moquette. Loop pile cloth, usually wool pile and cotton ground, used for upholstery.

Mordant. Substance used for fixing colours in dyeing.

Moser. Brushing machine for cloth.

Mule. Woollen spinning machine with spindles on moving carriage; largely superseded by the woollen ring frame.

Mungo. Material recovered from new or old hard-woven or milled cloth and felt.

Nap. Fibrous surface raised on the surface of some cloths such as flannel.

Nep. Small knot of entangled fibres.

Noble comb. Machine normally used in the Bradford worsted trade.

Noil. Short fibres rejected by the comb; this material commonly passes from the worsted to the woollen section of the industry.

Nun's veiling. Light-weight, plain-weave cloth usually dyed black.

Oil-combed tops. Wool or hair tops containing added oil.

Oleine. Oil consisting mainly of free oleic acid used in woollen processing.

Optical bleaching (*brightening*, *whitening*) *agent*. Terms sometimes used for *Fluorescent brightening agent*.

Papermaker's felt. Cloth used on paper-making machine for supporting the wet pulp.

Perching. Examination of cloth for faults before finishing; the cloth is drawn over a "perch" or long roller sited near a good north or artificial light.

Persian lamb. The pelt (skin and wool complete) from Karakul lambs slaughtered when they are a few days old and the ringlets are still tight and curly.

pH. Scale for expressing the acidity or alkalinity of a solution.

Pick. A thread or group of threads carried across the warp during one passage of the shuttle.

Piece. Length of finished cloth. (Used also in plural to denote small inferior pieces of the fleece.)

Piece scouring. Process of cleansing the cloth after weaving and before finishing.

Pilling. Accumulation of small clusters of entangled fibres on the surface of a cloth.

Pirn. Wooden, plastic, or paper spool on which weft yarn is wound for weaving.

Ply. The number of folded yarns in a cabled yarn.

Potting. Finishing process mainly for woollen cloth: somewhat similar to crabbing.

Pulling. Process for opening up rags before further processing. Used also to denote the removal of wool from skins.

Quality. Property of wool assessed mainly from the fineness of the fibres.

Rags. New rags are surplus cloth from weaving, cutting out of garments, and unwanted patterns. Old rags are from discarded garments or similar material.

Raising. Production of nap on the surface of cloth by brushing or teasling.

Reaching-in. Drawing the warp threads through the heald eyes of a loom before drawing-in preparatory to weaving.

Reed. Frame of wires in a loom through which the warp threads pass; it serves to keep the warp threads properly spaced, and is used to beat up each weft thread after it has passed through the warp.

Reeling. The process of unwinding yarn from cops or bobbins and rewinding them on to a reel in the form of hanks.

Regain. The weight of moisture in a sample of wool expressed as a percentage of the oven-dry weight.

Relative humidity. A measure of the amount of moisture in the atmosphere, usually in a processing or testing room, expressed as a percentage.

Re-processed wool. Wool recovered from new cloth (see *Rags*).

Resist printing. Process in which a design is printed on the cloth with a substance which resists the dye in a subsequent dyeing.

Re-used wool. Wool recovered from old cloth (see *Rags*).

Ring Spinning. Method of spinning in which drafting, twisting, and winding-on are done simultaneously and continuously.

Roving. Final stage of worsted drawing before spinning.

Saxony. Fine quality tweed with smooth and soft handle, made largely in Scotland and the West of England (the wool now comes normally from Australia and South Africa).

Scouring. See *Piece scouring* and *Wool scouring*.

Scribbler. The first part of a woollen carding machine.

Selvedge (*list*). Side edge of a piece of cloth.

Serge. Piece-dyed cloth of twill weave.

Shalloon. Twilled wool cloth used for linings.

Shearling. A sheep, normally between 1 and 2 years old, that has been shorn only once.

Shed. Opening between warp threads through which the weft passes during weaving.

Shives. Vegetable matter in wool.

Shoddy. Material recovered by pulling new or old knitted or loosely woven fabrics.

Shrink-resistant. Describes material whose dimensional stability conforms to certain standards.

Skin wool. Wool removed from the skins of slaughtered sheep.

Skirtings. Stained and inferior parts of fleece set aside in shearing.

Slipe. Skin wool removed from skin by steeping in lime.

Sliver. Loose strand of fibres without twist.

Slub. Defect in yarn in the form of a thick place.

Slubbing. Strand of fibres being drawn from tops preparatory to worsted spinning. Also the product of the woollen card ready for spinning.

Spool. Wooden former on which weft yarn is wound for weaving.

Standard atmosphere. An atmosphere (as, for example, often laid down for testing) with a relative humidity of 65 per cent and a temperature of 20°C (68°F).

Standard condition. Condition of material that has reached equilibrium with the standard atmosphere—usually in preparation for some physical test.

Standard regain. *Regain* (q.v.) laid down for wool in various forms for buying and selling purposes.

Staple. Tuft of fibres grown together in the fleece.

Suint. Excretions from sweat glands of sheep.

Tear. Ratio of top to noil produced in combing (pronounced *tare*).

Teasel gig. Machine for raising nap on surface of cloth.

Tegg wool. See *Hogg wool*.

Tender wool. Wool having less than normal tensile strength.

Tenter. Machine for drying cloth and also for removing creases and straightening before further processing.

Tex. System based on metric units recommended by the International Organization for Standardization (ISO) for universal use in describing the linear density of textile yarns.

Thrums. Surplus ends of cloth, or of warp only, from weaving.

Tippy wool. Wool in which the tips of the fibres have been damaged by natural weathering on the sheep to such an extent that dyeing is affected.

Top (*tops*). Sliver of fibres produced by the comb in worsted processing (the "raw material" of the worsted spinner).

Tweed. Originally a cloth made in the Tweed area, the term is now used for a variety of woollen cloths having effects produced by colour and weave.

Twill. Diagonal lines on the face of a woven cloth; also applied to a cloth so woven.

Vicuna. Undercoat of the vicuna, a type of llama; it produces remarkably soft and fine quality cloths.

Vigoureux printing. See *Melange printing.*

Virgin wool. New and unused wool.

Warp. Threads running lengthways in a cloth.

Warp knitting. Whereas in ordinary ("weft") knitting only one thread is used, in warp knitting at least one thread is supplied to every needle.

Warping. Process of arranging warp yarns in preparation for weaving.

Washing-off. Treatment in water or detergent solution to remove substances used in previous process.

Weft. Threads running widthways in cloth.

Weft knitting. Method of knitting with a single thread in which loops are formed across the width of the fabric.

Willey (*willow*). There are many types of willey, with alternative and local names, for opening greasy wool and also for preliminary blending.

Wilton. Carpet somewhat similar to Brussels but with cut pile, and usually of superior quality.

Wool classing. The dividing of whole fleeces into separate classes; usually done on the sheep station or farm.

Wool scouring. The cleansing of raw or loose wool before such preliminary mechanical processes as carding.

Wool sorting. The separation and grading of fleece wool into various qualities.

Note

For a fuller glossary of textile terms the reader is referred to the Textile Institute's book *Textile Terms and Definitions.*

Name Index

205

Subject Index

FARNHAM SCHOOL OF ART